# How to Use This Book

## Look for these special features in this book:

**SIDEBARS**, **CHARTS**, **GRAPHS**, and original **MAPS** expand your understanding of what's being discussed—and also make useful sources for classroom reports.

**FAQs** answer common **F**requently **A**sked **Q**uestions about people, places, and things.

**WOW FACTORS** offer "Who knew?" facts to keep you thinking.

**TRAVEL GUIDE** gives you tips on exploring the state—either in person or right from your chair!

**PROJECT ROOM** provides fun ideas for school assignments and incredible research projects. Plus, there's a guide to primary sources—what they are and how to cite them.

Please note: All statistics are as up-to-date as possible at the time of publication.

Consultant: Linda K. Harvey, Special Collections Librarian, Alabama State University; William Loren Katz; Maurice A. Meylan, Professor of Geology, University of Southern Alabama

Book production by The Design Lab

Library of Congress Cataloging-in-Publication Data
Somervill, Barbara A.
    Alabama / by Barbara A. Somervill.
        p. cm.—(America the beautiful. Third series)
    Includes bibliographical references and index.
    ISBN-13: 978-0-531-18556-8
    ISBN-10: 0-531-18556-7
    1. Alabama—Juvenile literature. I. Title. II. Series.
    F326.3.S66 2008
    976.1—dc22                              2006037697

AMERICA ★ THE ★ BEAUTIFUL

# Alabama

BY BARBARA A. SOMERVILL

Third Series

Children's Press®
An Imprint of Scholastic Inc.
New York ★ Toronto ★ London ★ Auckland ★ Sydney
Mexico City ★ New Delhi ★ Hong Kong
Danbury, Connecticut

# CONTENTS

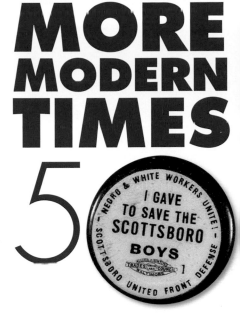

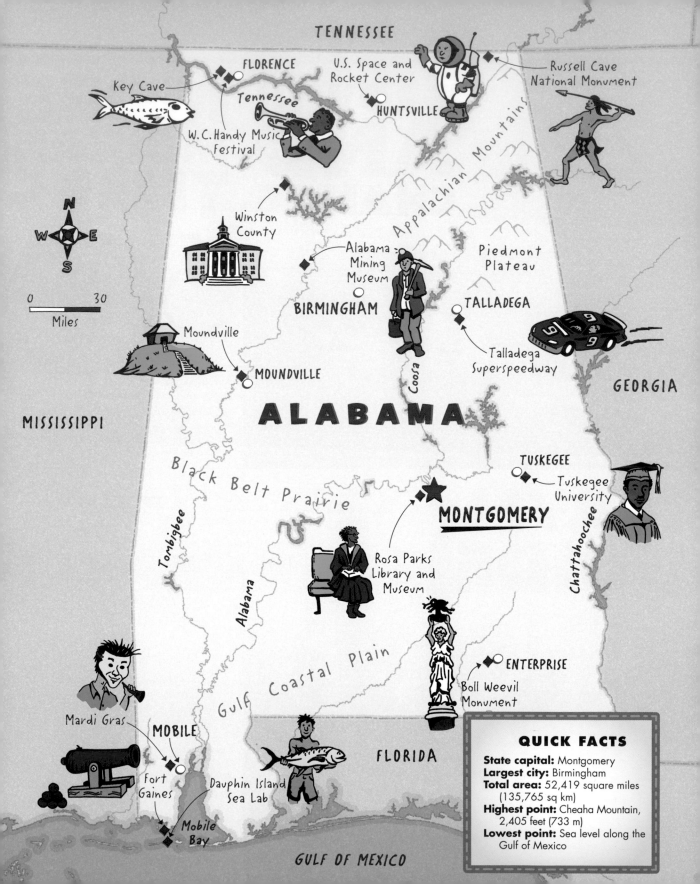

TENNESSEE

Key Cave

FLORENCE

W.C. Handy Music Festival

U.S. Space and Rocket Center

HUNTSVILLE

Russell Cave National Monument

Tennessee

Appalachian Mountains

Winston County

Alabama Mining Museum

Piedmont Plateau

BIRMINGHAM

TALLADEGA

Talladega Superspeedway

N
W    E
S

0     30
Miles

Moundville

MOUNDVILLE

Coosa

ALABAMA

GEORGIA

MISSISSIPPI

Black Belt Prairie

TUSKEGEE

Tuskegee University

MONTGOMERY

Chattahoochee

Tombigbee

Alabama

Rosa Parks Library and Museum

Gulf Coastal Plain

ENTERPRISE

Boll Weevil Monument

Mardi Gras

MOBILE

FLORIDA

Fort Gaines

Dauphin Island Sea Lab

Mobile Bay

GULF OF MEXICO

QUICK FACTS

**State capital:** Montgomery
**Largest city:** Birmingham
**Total area:** 52,419 square miles (135,765 sq km)
**Highest point:** Cheaha Mountain, 2,405 feet (733 m)
**Lowest point:** Sea level along the Gulf of Mexico

# Welcome to Alabama!

## HOW ALABAMA GOT ITS NAME

On the southeastern border of what is now the United States there lived a people called Alibamu, whose name was made of two words: *alba* (which means "plants" or "vegetation") and *amo* (which means "gatherer" or "picker"). The description "plant gatherer" fits the Alibamu, who cleared land to create their villages. The Alabama River was named for these people by European explorers in the 16th century, who used a slightly different spelling. Eventually part of this region became known by the same name, Alabama.

ALABAMA

ATLANT.
OCEAN

FLORIDA

8

## READ
## ABOUT

A channel through
a bayou near
Bayou La Batre

CHAPTER ONE

# LAND

★

A LABAMA'S A PLACE OF HOT AND HUMID DAYS AND SULTRY NIGHTS. Its 52,419 square miles (135,765 square kilometers) are made of lush and beautiful hills, mountains, waterways, and bustling cities teeming with diverse people. In the hot and humid summers, the average temperature can reach 90 degrees Fahrenheit (32 degrees Celsius) near the Gulf of Mexico, Alabama's lowest point at sea level. Winters are cool and mild with an average January temperature of 51°F (10°C). Except for its highest point, Cheaha Mountain, at 2,405 feet (733 meters), Alabama rarely sees snow.

Gulf State Park is part of Alabama's coastal region.

## WORD TO KNOW

**sediment** *material eroded from rocks and deposited elsewhere by wind, water, or glaciers*

# IN THE BEGINNING

Millions of years ago, the region known as Alabama was mostly tropical, and the land was much lower. The Gulf of Mexico was larger than it is now. It covered the land with warm water, rich with clams, mussels, and other sea life. The waters ebbed, the sea life died, and a layer of shells and dead sea creatures collected on what had been the seafloor. Over the next several million years, the land went through many changes. Mountains formed and then eroded, sending **sediment** down into the lowlands and covering the sea-shell-skeleton layer. Over time, the increasingly heavy sediment created pressure, which turned the dead sea creatures into limestone.

This pattern of seawater and sediment covering sea skeletons was repeated several times. At one point, seas buried dense young forests, eventually turning them into coal deposits. By the beginning of the Cenozoic period, about 65 million years ago, Alabama was covered with trees and plants that grew nearly year-round. Then saltwater seas gave way to encroaching ice.

The ice age changed the climate. Colder weather changed the amount and type of **precipitation**. It also changed animal and plant species living in an area. Pine forests replaced rain forests. Megafauna—huge beasts—such as mammoths, mastodons, and giant sloths rambled over the landscape. The push of **glaciers** from the north also encouraged clans of people to move south. These hunters and gatherers followed game trails, arriving in what is now Alabama roughly 14,000 years ago.

**Q8 WHY DID ALABAMA CHOOSE A WHALE AS ITS STATE FOSSIL?**

**A8** A fossil of *Basilosaurus cetoides*, an early version of a whale, was unearthed on a plantation in southwestern Alabama in 1834. *Basilosaurus* lived in the Gulf of Mexico about 40 million to 50 million years ago.

# Alabama Geo-Facts

Along with the state's geographical highlights, this chart ranks Alabama's land, water, and total area compared to all other states.

**Total area; rank** . . . . . . . 52,419 square miles (135,765 sq km); 30th
**Land; rank** . . . . . . . . . . . 50,744 square miles (131,426 sq km); 28th
**Water; rank** . . . . . . . . . . . . 1,675 square miles (4,338 sq km); 23rd
**Inland water; rank** . . . . . . . . 956 square miles (2,476 sq km); 23rd
**Coastal water; rank** . . . . . . . 519 square miles (1,344 sq km); 12th
**Territorial water; rank** . . . . . . . 200 square miles (518 sq km); 18th
**Geographic center** . . . Chilton, 12 miles (19 km) southwest of Clanton
**Latitude** . . . . . . . . . . . . . . . . . . . . . . . . . . 84° 51′ N to 88° 28′ N
**Longitude** . . . . . . . . . . . . . . . . . . . . . . . . 30° 13′ W to 35° W
**Highest point** . . . . . . . . . . . . Cheaha Mountain, 2,405 feet (733 m)
**Lowest point** . . . . . . . . . . . . . . . . . . Sea level at the Gulf of Mexico
**Largest city** . . . . . . . . . . . . . . . . . . . . . . . . . . . . . . Birmingham
**Longest river** . . . . . . . . . . . . . . . . . . . . . . . . . . . . . . . Alabama

Source: U.S. Census Bureau

**Alabama is the 30th-largest state, roughly equal in size to New York, Arkansas, or Louisiana. The state of Delaware would fit inside it about 26 times.**

# Alabama Topography

Use the color-coded elevation chart to see on the map Alabama's high points (orange) and low points (green to dark green). Elevation is measured as the distance above or below sea level.

## LAND REGIONS

Most of Alabama never rises above 500 feet (150 m), but hills and valleys cut through the northeast. On the other side of the mountainous northern border lies Tennessee. A section of the Florida Panhandle juts along the state's southern border, leaving Alabama with 53 miles (85 km) of coastline. Alabama lies east of Mississippi and west of Georgia. North to south, Alabama measures 332 miles (534 km), while east to west covers 191 miles (307 km). You could drive across the state in about three hours.

On the southern coast, Alabama boasts sunny, sandy beaches, while in the north it offers steep ridges and limestone valleys. And there is lots of farm country—and timber country. The state is divided into five to seven major regions, depending on whom you ask and what part of the land is being studied. Those regions include the Cumberland Plateau, the Valley and Ridge, the Blue Ridge, the Piedmont, and the Gulf Coastal Plain. The other

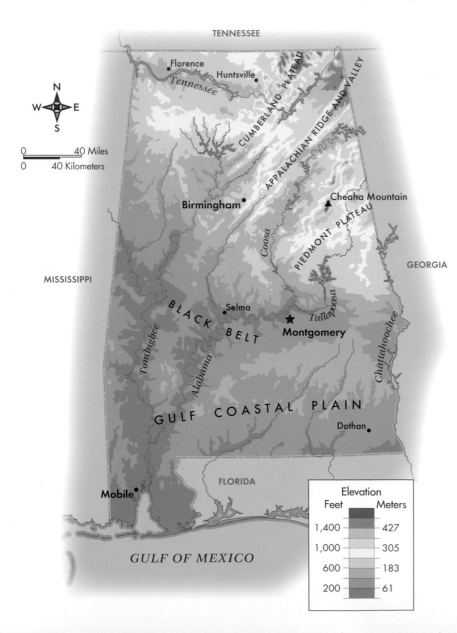

TENNESSEE

Florence
Huntsville

*Tennessee*

CUMBERLAND PLATEAU

APPALACHIAN RIDGE AND VALLEY

N
W E
S

0      40 Miles
0    40 Kilometers

Birmingham

▲ Cheaha Mountain

PIEDMONT PLATEAU

*Coosa*

GEORGIA

MISSISSIPPI

B L A C K

Selma

*Tallapoosa*

B E L T

★ Montgomery

*Chattahoochee*

*Tombigbee*

*Alabama*

GULF    COASTAL    PLAIN

Dothan

FLORIDA

Mobile

| Elevation | |
|---|---|
| Feet | Meters |
| 1,400 | 427 |
| 1,000 | 305 |
| 600 | 183 |
| 200 | 61 |

*GULF OF MEXICO*

sections—the Black Belt Prairie and the Interior Low Plateau—have more to do with the rich dark soil than topographical features.

## The Cumberland Plateau

This region is at the tail end of the Appalachian Mountain range, which runs from Maine to northeast Alabama. This mountain range is old and weathered, so its peaks are not very high. The Cumberland Plateau, also known as the Appalachian Plateau, has rolling hills, sandstone ridges, valleys, and the ever-present Alabama red clay soil, which is red because of its high iron content. Limestone caverns dot the region and offer a fascinating underground world for visitors. Sequoyah Caverns and Cathedral Caverns feature eerie **stalactite** and **stalagmite** formations.

Alabama's **DeSoto Caverns** were used as a burial ground for the people of the Woodland culture about 2,000 years ago!

### WORDS TO KNOW

**stalactite** *a column or pillar formed on the roof of a cave from dripping groundwater*

**stalagmite** *a column or pillar formed on the floor of a cave from dripping groundwater*

Hikers explore the forest trails in Monte Sano State Park.

Pulpit Rock on Cheaha Mountain looks out over Cheaha Mountain State Park.

**Dismalites emit a bright blue-green light to attract flying insects, which they eat in large numbers!**

## SEE IT HERE!

### DISMALS CANYON

Several hundred years ago, Native Americans held sacred ceremonies in Dismals Canyon. A couple hundred years ago, outlaws used the canyon as a hideout. Today, you can hike, canoe, and camp among Dismals Canyon's caves and waterfalls. You might even see glow-in-the-dark creatures (glowworms), which locals call dismalites after the canyon's name.

## The Valley and Ridge

This region is also the tail end of the Appalachian Mountain range. Here the Coosa and Tallapoosa rivers wind through forested valleys, eventually joining the Alabama River to the southwest. Iron ore mining is done throughout this area, especially near Birmingham, Alabama's largest city. The fact that large-scale mining of iron ore has occurred here for years is one reason why Birmingham has grown to be Alabama's largest, wealthiest city.

## The Blue Ridge

The state's highest point, Cheaha Mountain in the Talladega National Forest, is in this region, which is also called the Talladega Range and the Appalachian Ridge.

## The Piedmont

Landforms change dramatically from Alabama's mountainous northeast to the foothills of the Piedmont district and the Gulf Coastal Plain. "Piedmont" means foot (*pied*) of the mountain (*mont*), so it's no surprise that this area is made up of low hills and broad valleys. Lying along the middle of Alabama's eastern border, it is part of the Appalachian Mountain range. The area is rich in iron ore and manganese, two minerals mined heavily in Alabama. The Piedmont region was also extensively mined for gold in the early 19th century and served as one of America's main gold prospecting sites before the California gold rush. Along the eastern edge of the Piedmont, the Chattahoochee River marks the border with Georgia.

A view of the Talladega National Forest in the Piedmont region

A paddle boat travels up the Black Warrior River.

### The Gulf Coastal Plain

This region borders, you guessed it, the Alabama coast. It actually takes up the southern half of Alabama. Land in the Gulf Coastal Plain is flat, with a few low ridges, and much of the soil is sandy. To the west, the Upper Tombigbee River and the Black Warrior River meet to form the Lower Tombigbee, a body of water that empties into Mobile Bay.

Along the southern border of Alabama are wetlands, or swamps. They and the organisms that live in them clean the water, filtering out pollutants and keeping a balance of nutrients in it. Wetlands provide a nursery for many fish and bird species. For hundreds of years, Alabama's wetlands were filled in with soil or drained to create farmland. Nearly half of Alabama's natural wetlands were lost to agriculture through damming and draining. Today, Alabama is trying to reverse the loss of valuable wetlands. The 1966 and 1996 federal farm bills included "Swampbuster" provisions that bar farmers from any financial support if they drain, dredge, fill, level, or otherwise change a wetland area.

## REGIONAL SUBDIVISIONS

Parts of Alabama fall into two other regional categories based mostly on their soil. These areas consist of plenty of rich Alabama farmland and have been a big part of Alabama's agricultural success.

### The Black Belt Prairie

The Black Belt Prairie is a crescent-shaped region that runs for about 300 miles (480 km) through Tennessee, Georgia, Alabama, and Mississippi. The Black Belt is known for rich, dark soil, which makes it perfect land for farming and agriculture.

In the early 19th century, plantation owners, particularly in Alabama and Mississippi, chose the Black Belt Prairie region for their cotton plantations. They also planted crops such as rice, sugar, and tobacco. Today, most of the Black Belt is farmland, with a range of crops being grown, including most of the nation's peanuts and soybeans.

A peanut crop being harvested on a farm in Geneva

## ALONG THE CAHABA RIVER

The Cahaba is home to unique plants, river creatures, and insects. This is a look-but-don't-touch environment. The Cahaba supports 69 rare and threatened species, including fish and mussels found on the federal endangered species list. The Cahaba shiner, a fish once abundant in the river, is now found in just a short 15-mile (24 km) stretch of the Cahaba. Along the banks of the slow-moving river, look for the Cahaba lily, a threatened flower species.

### WORD TO KNOW

**shoals** *sandbanks or sandbars that make water shallow*

**Cahaba lilies**

### The Interior Low Plateau

This area includes land along the Tennessee border. This is farming country, with rich, fertile clay soil. The plateau covers both sides of the Tennessee River valley. The Tennessee River cuts through the northern tip of Alabama. Alabama's largest lake, Guntersville Lake, which is 108 square miles (280 sq km), was formed by damming the Tennessee. Alabama has only human-made lakes.

Along its 190 miles (305 km), the Cahaba River splashes over rocky **shoals** through the ridges and valleys. Farther south, it slows and gently wanders through cypress swamps and coastal plains. Toward the end of its journey, the Cahaba joins the Alabama River.

There is plenty to learn from this unique freshwater environment. In 1992, eight new plant species were identified along the Little Cahaba branch of the main river. And someone spotted a Septima's clubtail dragonfly along the Cahaba in 2002—the first Alabama sighting of this rare insect in 50 years. No one knows what other plants and animals might live along these quiet Alabama waters.

### CLIMATE

Alabama's regions can also be divided by climate. The divisions include the lower coastal plain, the upper coastal plain, and the northern plateau.

The lower coastal plain tends toward a subtropical climate that is strongly influenced by the warm waters of the Gulf of Mexico. The southern region has hot, humid summers and dramatic thunderstorms. Winters are relatively short and mild. Mobile, the largest city in this region, sees summer temperatures sizzle with an average high of 91°F (33°C) in July. Mobile experiences an average low temperature of 41°F (5°C) in January. Mobile is one of the rainiest cities in the United States. Average yearly precipitation (mostly rain) is 66.3 inches (168 centimeters).

The upper coastal plain, including the area of the Black Belt, also has long, hot summers and relatively mild winters. Birmingham's weather represents the standard of this region. Birmingham's average July high temperature is 90°F (32°C) and its average January low temperature is about 34°F (2°C). Yearly, Birmingham expects about a foot less rain than Mobile usually gets, but can also get snow.

## HURRICANES AND THUNDERSTORMS

Alabama residents expect to get hit by at least one hurricane a year. Located on the Gulf of Mexico, where many hurricanes strike land, Alabama prepares for heavy winds, pelting rain, flooding, and the problems that result from that combination.

Hurricanes and tropical storms vary in the speed of their winds and the amount

# Weather Report

TEMPERATURE **112°F**    TEMPERATURE **-27°F**

This chart shows record temperatures (high and low) for the state, as well as average temperatures (January and July) and average annual precipitation.

**Record high temperature** . . . . . . . . . . . . . . . . . . . . . 112°F (44°C)
    at Centreville on September 5, 1925
**Record low temperature** . . . . . . . . . . . . . . . . . . . . –27°F (–33°C)
    at New Market on January 30, 1966
**Average July temperature** . . . . . . . . . . . . . . . . . . . 82°F (28°C)
**Average January temperature** . . . . . . . . . . . . . . . . 51°F (10°C)
**Average annual precipitation** . . . . . . . . . . . . 66 inches (168 cm)

Source: National Climatic Data Center, NESDIS, NOAA, U.S. Department of Commerce

of rain they carry. No two hurricanes are alike, but you can expect major inconvenience with every one. When a powerful hurricane is on the way, Alabamians leave the coast and move inland. Thousands of vehicles clog the roads, hopefully ahead of the storm's edge. When the hurricane strikes, winds knock down trees, rip shutters and shingles from homes, and send loose items, such as lawn decorations, through the air like missiles. The wind also pushes the gulf waters, and a storm surge—a wave of water—may swamp roads and buildings along the coast.

Recent hurricanes that had a serious effect on Alabama include Danny in 1997, Ivan in 2004, and Katrina in 2005. Danny was perhaps the most unusual hurricane of the bunch. Danny arrived at Mobile and stopped moving. It sat and sat, dumping a massive amount of water on the city. Ivan brought floods to Gulf Shores with a rather strange result. The local zoo had

Gulf State Pier in Gulf Shores during Hurricane Isidore in 2002

Damaged boats sit on the shore at Bayou La Batre following Hurricane Katrina in 2005.

failed to evacuate its six alligators, which escaped in the high water. Chuckie, a 12-foot (3.7 m), 1,000-pound (455 kilogram) male, was among the escapees.

In 2005, Hurricane Katrina swept over New Orleans, Louisiana, and destroyed much of the city. Few Americans were aware of Katrina's affect on the Gulf Coast of Alabama, however. The town of Bayou La Batre was devastated, and its shrimping business was completely wiped out. Millions of dollars in damage to homes, buildings, and roadways occurred in the coastal region of the state. Alabamians quickly went to the aid of their fellow citizens, and rebuilding has restored much of the area.

Although hurricanes are powerful, they lack the electric vitality of an Alabama thunderstorm. Hot, sultry nights give way to distant rumbling. As the sound comes closer, flashes of lightning fill the sky. Windows rattle and rain rat-a-tats on the roof. Thunder rolls and lightning flashes at the same time. Within minutes the storm moves away, but for those few moments, the sudden summer storm has added drama to the Alabama landscape.

**WOW**

**Hurricane Danny dumped a record amount of rain on Alabama. The Dauphin Island Sea Lab recorded a remarkable 25.98 inches (66 cm) of rain in seven hours and 36.71 inches (93 cm) of rain during the entire storm!**

## FAQ

**Q: WHAT IS A YELLOWHAMMER?**

**A:** A yellowhammer, or flicker, is the state bird of Alabama. A member of the woodpecker family, the yellowhammer has brown feathers with black markings. The underside of the wings and the tail are bright yellow.

forests teemed with huge bison, oversized bears, elk, and deer. Hunting eliminated all but the deer. Small mammals common to just about every North American forest also live in Alabama, including raccoons, opossums, rabbits, and squirrels. Red and gray foxes join Florida panthers, bobcats, beavers, muskrats, and a full range of weasels.

An intensive conservation campaign saved Alabama's white-tailed deer and wild turkey populations. In 1940, population counts showed only 14,108 white-tailed deer and 11,600 wild turkeys. Since then, controlled hunting has allowed these animal populations to grow. Alabama forests now provide a home for 1.4 million deer and 350,000 wild turkeys.

### MINI-BIO

### BLANCHE EVANS DEAN: CONSERVATION QUEEN

For nearly 30 years, Blanche Evans Dean (1892–1974) taught biology in Alabama public schools. Dean impressed on her students a love of nature, including birds, insects, trees, and flowers. Dean established the Alabama State Nature Camp as a way to help teachers learn about natural history and conservation. She founded several conservation societies during her lifetime, including the Alabama Wildlife Society and the Alabama Conservancy. In 1985, Dean was inducted into the Alabama Women's Hall of Fame.

**? Want to know more?** See www.awhf.org/dean.html

Red foxes are among the many mammals found in Alabama's woodlands.

Workers clean up a diesel fuel spill after Hurricane Katrina.

## PROTECTING THE ENVIRONMENT

What keeps the air clean, the rivers running clear, and the soil rich? It's efforts by environmentalists and volunteers who work hard to keep forest preserves, river ways, and natural parks and areas clean from litter and pollution. But it's not easy, and it takes the extra effort of all citizens to keep the state clean. With the growth of industries in the South, and particularly in Alabama cities like Birmingham and Montgomery, it is becoming increasingly difficult to keep the state as beautiful as it has always been. But the people of the state are dedicated to protecting and preserving their "Sweet Home Alabama."

## ENDANGERED SPECIES

Alabama has 117 species of animals, fish, and birds on the U.S. Fish & Wildlife Service list of threatened and endangered species. Humpback whales, bald eagles, and wood storks are making a comeback, thanks to popular support in terms of interest and money. It is much harder to get people interested in the Alabama beach mouse, which lives among the sandy coastal dunes, or any one of several dozen endangered mussels and snails.

Two species of beach mouse and the Alabama cavefish are both on the endangered species list and they also live in critically endangered habitats. As beach areas draw more tourists, coastal dune habitats become overpopulated. People tromp across the dunes, dump their garbage along the coast, and interfere with the dwellings of the tiny mice. The only way to stop the problem is to stop human traffic. Local and national organizations are helping to preserve these habitats and the plants and animals that live in the dunes.

The Alabama cavefish is found in only one place—Key Cave in northwest Alabama. The fish swim in total darkness, and their bodies have adapted to their environment. The fish are pale skinned and blind. They are also exceedingly rare and difficult to study.

26

Thousands of years ago, people lived in Russell Cave, which is now a national monument in Jackson County.

**c. 28,000 BCE**
*Early people cross the Bering Land Bridge*

▲ **c. 10,500 BCE**
*The first humans arrive in what is now Alabama and hunt big game animals*

**c. 6500**
*Humans begin occupying Russell Cave*

# CHAPTER TWO

# FIRST PEOPLE

★

D URING A LONG ICE AGE ABOUT 30,000 YEARS AGO, MUCH OF THE EARTH'S WATER WAS HELD IN ICE. Sea levels were much lower, and a land bridge appeared between what is now Asia and North America. It became a kind of highway for people and animals to travel onto the North American continent.

**300 BCE–1000 CE**

*The Woodland culture exists*

**800–900**

*Height of the Choctaw civilization*

▲**900–1500**

*Mound Builders thrive in the region*

## ENTERING ALABAMA

Slowly, over thousands of years, the hunter-gatherers moved to the southeast, arriving in what is now Alabama in about 10,500 BCE. Following herds of animals that they hunted for food, they lived in temporary villages and shelters, or set up a base in a cave. Humans resided in one cave, now a national monument known as Russell Cave, for thousands of years. They left behind a record of their existence through artifacts such as spearheads, fishhooks, bones, and pottery. These objects give **anthropologists** clues about how these people lived from 6500 BCE to 1650 CE, including what they hunted, ate, and made.

These early Americans lived in villages of 50 to 150 people. The men went on long-range hunting trips, while the women raised the children, collected other foods, and maintained the clan's most precious possession—fire! Fire kept people warm, protected them from animal attacks, and allowed them to cook their food.

### WORD TO KNOW

**anthropologists** *people who study the development of human cultures*

Huge animals such as the mastodon roamed Alabama more than 10,000 years ago.

# THE WOODLAND PEOPLE

In 1951, **archaeologists** discovered a scattering of ancient camps along the Tennessee River. They found tools made of animal bones and rock, as well as other artifacts. By studying them and their locations in the soil, scientists learned that hunting shifted from huge beasts to deer, rabbits, squirrels, raccoons, and birds. The people began to settle near rivers and streams because those locations attracted game and provided fresh water. Hunters became fishers, taking advantage of the plentiful fish, clams, and mussels.

The people became less nomadic, settling in a particular area during certain seasons because there was an adequate supply of game and water available. Though they still depended on berries, nuts, and roots that had to be gathered, over time, they began to plant and harvest crops, growing beans, squash, and corn. At that time, an ear of corn didn't have the neat, uniform rows of yellow or white kernels that we find in supermarkets today. It was coarse, multicolored corn that could be hulled, dried, and cooked into a mush during long, chilly winters.

Planting crops and living in larger groups are activities associated with what archaeologists term the Woodland stage. The Woodland culture in what is now Alabama existed from about 300 BCE to 1000 CE.

## WORD TO KNOW

**archaeologists** *people who study the remains of past human societies*

# W★W

**The changes from hunter-gatherers to Woodland people and then from Woodland to Mississippian cultures took place gradually, and the time period during which each culture existed overlapped with the next.**

Native corn was multicolored with irregular rows of kernels.

## SEE IT HERE!

### MOUNDVILLE

A thousand years ago, people of the Mississippian culture settled along the Black Warrior River in Alabama. These people, called the Mound Builders today, built a square town protected by a tall wooden fence. Once a thriving city, Moundville had a central plaza and two massive earth mounds used for religious events. The Mound Builders built 26 mounds, some of which were shaped like flat-topped pyramids. Today, the area is overgrown with grass, and the sides of the main mound are tree-covered. Archaeologists have uncovered pottery, jewelry, and other artifacts that help them understand the lives of the Mound Builders.

# MOUND BUILDERS

Between 900 and 1500 CE, a new culture evolved. Unlike any other people in the region before, these people created huge earthen pyramids and mounds. Because of this, they are sometimes called Mound Builders. Archaeologists call them Mississippians because the first evidence of their culture was found in the Mississippi River valley.

**MINI-BIO**

### CLARENCE BLOOMFIELD MOORE: UNCOVERING HISTORY

When Clarence Bloomfield Moore (1852–1936) began investigating the earthworks at Moundville, Alabama, he knew he'd found something special. Born in Philadelphia, Pennsylvania, Moore was an amateur archaeologist with a passionate interest in Native American Mound Builders, exploring mounds throughout the southern United States. His discovery of Moundville in 1905 was probably his greatest contribution to American archaeology. Today, Moundville is part of the University of Alabama. It is a significant archaeological park, where visitors can learn about the area's history and archaeologists continue to do research.

❓ Want to know more? See *The Moundville Expeditions of Clarence Bloomfield Moore* by Clarence B. Moore (Tuscaloosa: University of Alabama Press, 1996)

The Mound Builders grew a surplus of crops and thrived on a corn-based economy. They lived in cities, practiced religion, and organized themselves into social classes, with nobles ruling the community.

At its height, Moundville, a 300-acre (120-ha) village, housed about 1,000 people within its walls and served another 9,000 living in the nearby valley. The village consisted of a main plaza, 26 earth mounds, houses, and a place for preparing the dead for burial. The largest mound, a steep pyramid, stands 58.5 feet (17.8 m) high and served as a burial site.

Mounds that were built 1,000 years ago can still be seen at Moundville. The tallest of the mounds rises to a height of 58.5 feet (17.8 m).

# Native American Peoples

## (Before European Contact)

This map shows the general area of Native American peoples before European settlers arrived.

Choctaws perform a dance before beginning a ball game.

## ALABAMA'S NATIVE PEOPLE

For reasons no one knows, the Mississippian culture began to disappear. Eventually, dozens of new groups emerged. Although many small ones existed, five major cultures began to dominate the region: Alibamus, Chickasaws, Choctaws, Creeks, and Coushattas (Koasatis). Cherokee territory included today's Tennessee, Georgia, and the northeast corner of Alabama.

Most Native American peoples in Alabama cultivated community farm plots and lived in houses made of river cane and plaster, with thatched roofs. Each village had a circular town center for meetings and a field for a sport called lacrosse.

The men hunted and protected the villages. Villages banded together to fight intruders. Women cooked, sewed, and raised children. Men and women were storytellers, practiced medicine, and created art and music. Healing depended on the use of herbs and other plants. Native healers understood which plants

## FAQ

**Q8 WHAT DID NATIVE ALABAMIANS TELL STORIES ABOUT?**

**A8** Many Native Americans told stories about the creation of their groups, the origins of fire and corn, and their ancestors.

## NATIVE LANGUAGES

The Alibamu and Choctaw langauges share some similar words:

| | Alibamu Language | Choctaw Language |
|---|---|---|
| Bear | Nita | Nita |
| Dog | Ifa | Ofi |
| Mountain lion | Kowi | Koi |
| Owl | Ofolo | Ofunlo |
| Rabbit | Cokfi | Chukfi |
| Raccoon | Sawa | Shaui |
| Skunk | Kono | Koni |

# WOW

One Choctaw community preserved potatoes by slicing and drying them over hickory smoke. Although not fried, these potato slices were a lot like modern-day potato chips. This Choctaw group was called Ahi Apet Okla—the potato-eating people.

could be used to treat various conditions. For example, willow root was used to lower a fever.

Crops supplemented the main diets of meat and fish. Most groups from Alabama depended heavily on the "three sisters"—corn, beans, and squash—for survival. What they didn't eat fresh they dried so they could cook it months later.

Most Native men and boys wore loincloths made of deerskin. They also wore leggings to protect their legs from brush and thorns. Women and girls wore long skirts and tops made of animal skins or cloth. All wore moccasins on their feet and thick leather robes over their shoulders to keep warm in winter.

## CHOCTAWS

For Choctaws, the day began at dawn and ended at sundown. The days were measured by the sun, and night was simply a time for sleeping. Choctaws revered the sun god, called Hashtahli. The moon was Hashtahli's wife; the stars were their children. Choctaws developed an advanced calendar, tracking the movements of the sun and moon. Divided into 13 months, the Choctaw year consisted of 364 days. Month names matched what was ripe during a specific month or when food was scarce. The name of one month translates to "month of the peach," and another to "month of big famine." When the first frost arrived, Choctaws began a new year.

Family relationships were vital to Native Americans. Among Choctaws, mothers raised the girls to womanhood and boys until age 12 or 13. Considered her mother's daughter until marriage, a girl learned how to cook

Native Americans hunting deer at night

and preserve food, tan hides and sew them into clothes, and plant and raise crops. When a boy reached 12 or 13, his father presented him with a bow and arrows or a blowpipe and darts. It was time to train as a warrior. As with many Native cultures, hunting and protecting the tribe fell to the men.

## MUSKOGEE CREEKS

Muskogee Creeks were a loose **confederacy** of nations that spoke similar languages. These people did not call themselves Creeks, but were given the English name by settlers who noticed that they lived by streams and rivers. Based on that observation, nearly all Native American groups should have been called "Creeks"!

### WORD TO KNOW

**confederacy** *a group that is formed for shared support and common goals*

# Picture Yourself . . .

## Playing Lacrosse

You face your opponents on a long, open field. You hold long sticks firmly in each hand. Running, you scoop a leather ball from the ground, cup it between the two sticks, and then pass the ball on to another team member. The ball, made of deerskin, flies through the air and is captured by an opponent who races to make a goal in the opposite direction.

The double-stick version of lacrosse was popular among Cherokees and Chickasaws of Alabama. But this game was a bit more physical than the lacrosse of today. Tribes often fielded teams of 50, 100, and even 200 players, all on the field at the same time, all scrambling for one ball. That's rough play!

The Muskogee Creeks occupied almost the entire eastern half of today's Alabama. Various villages sprang up along the Coosa, Tallapoosa, Flint, and Chattahoochee rivers. In all, there seem to have been about 50 towns and six languages. Most Creeks enjoyed music, but among the men, the real passion was a version of lacrosse.

Choctaw men competing in a game of lacrosse

When a Creek child was born, he or she belonged to the mother's clan. Women ran the family; men ran the town. Within a town, the men elected a chief, called a *miko*. Like the president and governors of today, the *miko* had a council of advisers. The *miko* listened to the council and followed the opinions of the majority.

The Creeks' most important religious ceremony was the yearly *pushkita*, which celebrated the New Year. The council members and warriors met in a cone-shaped building called the great council house, which was sometimes up to 40 feet (12 m) in diameter. The men sat in a spiral, with the most important councilors at the center and the least important men at the end. This was a men-only affair—a place that excluded women and children. The men smoked tobacco and swapped tales of their heroic battles. Servants (men only) brought in a black drink, a beverage brewed from the leaves and roots the dahoon holly plant. At the center of the great council house, a new fire was lit, which marked the start of the New Year.

The lives of Native Americans changed when Europeans arrived in North America. In Alabama, the newcomers represented greed, brutality, deceit, and disease. It is little wonder that the Indians fought against the European invasion.

## WOW

When one team faced another across a lacrosse field, each team could consist of 200 players!

Tobacco pipe

## READ ABOUT

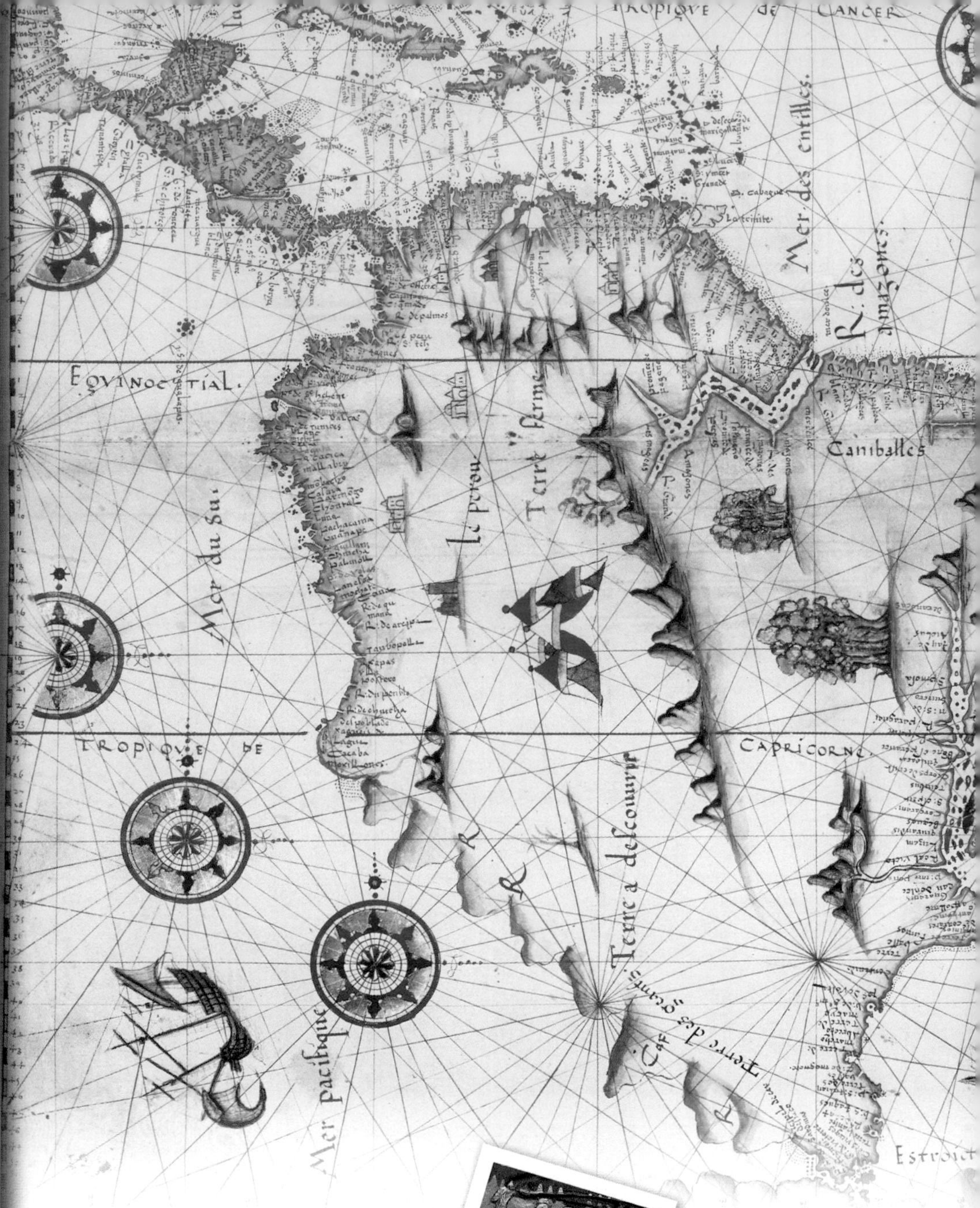

A map from the 1500s details the Atlantic coast of the Americas.

**1519**

*Alonzo de Piñeda sails into the Gulf of Mexico*

▲**1540**

*Hernando de Soto and Tuscaloosa (above) meet*

**1699**

*The Le Moyne brothe enter Mobile Bay*

# CHAPTER THREE

# EXPLORATION AND SETTLEMENT

★

GOLD! SILVER! JEWELS! Spanish explorers hoped to find El Dorado, or the city of gold, in North America. In 1519, Alonzo de Piñeda's ships sailed along the coast of the Gulf of Mexico. He sailed up rivers that fed into the gulf and visited about 40 Indian villages on his journey. Historians think Piñeda probably traveled into Mobile Bay. Much of his journal describes the towns of Alabama's Native people.

**1754 ▶**
*The French and Indian War begins*

**1763**
*Major Robert Farmer takes control of Mobile*

**1795**
*The Yazoo land sale takes place*

## MINI-BIO

## TUSCALOOSA: A RESPECTED LEADER

Tuscaloosa (also spelled Tuzcalusa; died 1540?) was a Choctaw chief. The name *Tuscaloosa* means "black warrior" in the Choctaw language and referred to Tuscaloosa's skill as a warrior and leader. Little is known about his life other than that when Hernando de Soto's Spanish expedition entered what is now Alabama, Tuscaloosa led the Choctaws in a bloody battle against de Soto's party. The present-day city of Tuscaloosa is named for this chief.

**? Want to know more?** See *Through Indian Eyes: the Untold Story of Native American Peoples* (Pleasantville, NY: Reader's Digest Association, 1995)

## SPANISH EXPLORERS

The first Europeans to live for any time in what is now Alabama were led by Hernando de Soto in 1540. De Soto was a typical Spanish conquistador (conqueror). To him, gold was everything. De Soto arrived on the coast of Florida in 1539 and headed north into present-day Georgia and the Carolinas. On his quest for wealth, de Soto ordered ruthless massacres. He entered Native villages as a guest and then stole everything of value. His men even robbed graves.

When de Soto entered Alabama, he met the Choctaw chief Tuscaloosa and took him hostage. Tuscaloosa promised great wealth if only de Soto would take him to Mabila. The people of Mabila ambushed the better equipped Spaniards. The Spanish had armor, guns, and horses, so de Soto's party was victorious, though it lost some men, horses, and supplies. Soon after the battle, de Soto's party left Alabama.

Hernando de Soto visited the village of Malvilla, shown below, in 1540.

# European Exploration of Alabama

The colored arrows on this map show the routes taken by explorers between 1519 and 1699.

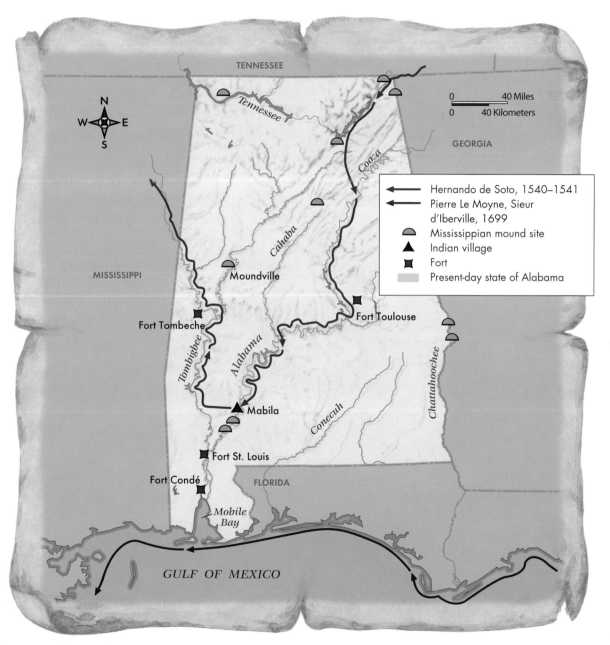

MINI-BIO

## JEAN-BAPTISTE LE MOYNE, SIEUR DE BIENVILLE: FOUNDER OF MOBILE

Born in Montreal, Jean-Baptiste Le Moyne, Sieur de Bienville (1680–1767), was a French Canadian explorer. When only 18, he joined his brother to help establish the French colony of Louisiana. By 1718, he had founded Mobile, Alabama, and New Orleans, Louisiana. Later, as governor of the region, Bienville developed an excellent relationship with Native Americans. He spoke several Indian dialects and treated both whites and Indians fairly.

**? Want to know more?** See http://international. loc.gov/intldl/fiahtml/fiatheme2c4.html

## Picture Yourself...

### in Fort Conde, Mobile

It is a scorching summer day, and you are wearing the woolen uniform of a French soldier. You are on lookout duty, in case the British attack. Being a soldier in the colonial days is hot, demanding work. You are on duty for long hours, get very little pay, and there are few, if any, holidays. The food is poor, unless you have enough money to supply your own. And you are probably very lonely, since you are far from home and communicating by letter takes months.

## FRENCH EXPLORERS

It was more than 150 years before the next European explorers, French brothers Pierre Le Moyne d'Iberville and Jean-Baptiste Le Moyne, Sieur de Bienville, arrived. In January 1699, they sailed into a place the French called La Mobilla, which was their name for what the Native people called present-day Mobile Bay. Bienville found the land around the bay appealing—lush with oaks, elms, pines, vines, and flowers. He built a fort on a bluff about 27 miles (43 km) upriver, including a guardhouse, a forge, a gunsmith workshop, and brick factory. In 1711, floods wiped out the original fort in what is now known as Old Mobile, and Bienville headed south to found the city of Mobile.

Despite Bienville's efforts, Mobile did not develop as a French settlement. Mobile never had more than a few hundred citizens, though it became the capital of French Louisiana. In 1718, Biloxi became the new capital, but the heart of French power lay in New Orleans, a center of trade on the southern end of the Mississippi River.

The Spanish and French settlers brought European clothes, guns, and horses, and planted new crops: oranges, figs, indigo, rice, and cotton. They introduced domestic livestock

Armed colonists travel through the mountains during the French and Indian War.

for food and as labor to help transport timber for lumber. But Europeans also brought deadly diseases—smallpox, measles, syphilis, and yellow fever. The Indians had no resistance to these diseases. Untold numbers of Native Americans died in epidemics.

## THE FRENCH AND INDIAN WAR

In 1754, the French and the British went to war over control of fur trapping and property rights in the Ohio Valley. Known as the Seven Years' War in Europe, it was called the French and Indian War in the colonies. The British battled the French and their Native American allies. France lost, and the Treaty of Paris of 1763 gave Mobile (and Alabama) to the British.

That year, British major Robert Farmer arrived in Mobile and took control of Fort Condé, which was renamed Fort Charlotte after the wife of the reigning king of England, George III.

Article 10.

The solemn Ratification of the present Treaty expedited in good and due Form shall be exchanged between the contracting Parties in the Space of six Months or sooner, if possible, to be computed from the Day of the Signature of the present Treaty. In Witness whereof We the undersigned their Ministers Plenipotentiary have in their Name and in Virtue of our full Powers, signed with our Hands the present Definitive Treaty, and caused the Seals of our Arms to be affixed thereto.

Done at Paris this third Day of September In the Year of our Lord, one thousand seven hundred and Eighty three.

D Hartley

John Adams

B Franklin

John Jay

The Treaty of Paris officially ended the American Revolution, recognizing the United States as a new nation.

# THE AMERICAN REVOLUTION

A dozen years later, the British found themselves at war with the 13 American colonies.

The American Revolution (1775–1783) freed the colonists from British control, but the Spanish freed Mobile. In 1780, Spaniards sailed from New Orleans (which was again under Spanish rule) and attacked Mobile's fort. British troops were stretched far too thin to save Mobile. When the Treaty of Paris of 1783 was signed, Great Britain gave Florida, which included Mobile at the time, back to Spain.

The part of the Mississippi Territory the United States gained from Great Britain included Alabama, but not Mobile. The new U.S. government surveyed and sold land gained from the British, ignoring the fact that Native peoples lived on that land. Then a flood of settlers headed into Alabama. "Alabama Fever"—the arrival of settlers— brought great changes to Alabama.

In 1795, the state of Georgia sold 40 million acres (16.2 million ha) of land, most of it in Alabama, for two and a half cents per acre. Speculators sold their land for one dollar per acre, making a massive profit. Settlers soon discovered they had been cheated.

By the early 1800s, Alabama's one-crop cotton economy had begun, an economy based on slave labor. Large plantations thrived in the fertile Alabama soil, and rich landowners grew wealthier. They owned the land, the crops, and also the African people who worked that land. Slavery was a bleak chapter in American history. It allowed southern landowners to prosper, while slaves plowed and planted, weeded and harvested. Cotton became a cruel king—a position it held into the early 1900s.

Harvesttime on a cotton plantation

## LAND FOR SALE . . . SORT OF

In 1795, the Georgia government sold about 40 million acres (16.2 million ha) of land to three land companies. This event was called the Yazoo land fraud after the name of two of the companies involved. The land was cheap, and much of it did not actually belong to Georgia, but to Alabama. Companies that purchased the land sold it at huge profits. President George Washington declared the sales illegal and sent U.S. troops to stop the sales.

An engraving shows Mobile and Mobile Bay as it would have appeared during the 1850s.

**1813**
*The Red Stick Creeks carry out a massacre at Fort Mims*

▲**1819**
*Alabama becomes a state*

**1830**
*Andrew Jackson signs the Indian Removal Act*

# CHAPTER FOUR

# GROWTH AND CHANGE

★

I N 1803, THE UNITED STATES PURCHASED THE LOUISIANA TERRITORY FROM FRANCE, DOUBLING THE SIZE OF THE COUNTRY. The United States believed that the purchase should include all of Alabama, but Spain disagreed. Spain held Florida and a part of southern Alabama, including the port of Mobile, and it was not about to give up this valuable seaport.

**1865**
*The Civil War ends*

**1867**
*U.S. Congress orders a constitutional convention in Alabama*

◄ **1861**
*Alabama secedes from the Union*

## MINI-BIO

### PUSHMATAHA: CHOCTAW LEADER

The Choctaw chief Pushmataha (1764–1824) was a courageous warrior and wise leader. He served as mingo (leader) of the Six Towns district and promoted friendly relationships with Europeans. In 1813, Pushmataha and 150 Choctaw warriors joined General Ferdinand Claiborne in an attack against the Creeks and the English at Kantchati, along the Alabama River. Pushmataha said, "The Creeks were once our friends. They have joined the English, and we must now follow different trails. When our fathers took the hand of [George] Washington, they told him the Choctaw would always be friends of his nation, and Pushmataha can not be false to their promises."

However, the U.S. government did not keep its promises to Choctaws. Pushmataha went to Washington, D.C., to protest the unfair treatment of his people to President Andrew Jackson, and died there in 1824.

❓ **Want to know more?** See *Biographical Dictionary of American Indian History to 1900* by Carl Waldman (New York: Facts on File, 2001)

## WORD TO KNOW

**prophet** *a person who knows God's will or can predict the future*

## BATTLING FOR CONTROL

By 1810, American planters living in Florida declared themselves independent of Spain. Two years later, in 1812, the Americans found themselves at war with Great Britain again. The Spanish allowed the British to use Mobile as a safe haven, which infuriated the U.S. government. In 1813, the U.S. Navy sailed into Mobile Bay, and Spain peacefully surrendered the fort. Mobile was the only land gained from the War of 1812.

## THE CREEK WAR

From the north came a Shawnee chief named Tecumseh, whom the Creeks regarded as a **prophet**. Tecumseh wanted to fight the whites and drive them from Native lands. He approached the Choctaw, led by Pushmataha, but they refused to join him. The Creeks, however, embraced Tecumseh's idea.

When Creeks tried to drive off white settlements, warfare ensued. In August 1813, Red Stick Creeks, led by William Weatherford (Chief Red Eagle), carried out an attack on Fort Mims. Terrified settlers demanded government protection.

Andrew Jackson and his troops defeated Creek warriors at the battle of Emucfau by the Tallapoosa River on January 22, 1814.

A major battle took place at Horseshoe Bend, with Tennessean Andrew Jackson attacking the Creek. With Cherokee, Choctaw, and Chickasaw warriors at his side, Jackson gained a decisive victory. The battle at Horseshoe Bend ended the Creek uprising, and Jackson gained a reputation as an Indian fighter. In the Treaty of Fort Jackson, Creeks gave up land to Jackson. Although they had fought alongside Jackson, Cherokees, Chickasaws, and Choctaws also were forced to sign treaties and surrender their land.

## INDIAN REMOVAL

In 1830, Andrew Jackson, as president of the United States, signed the Indian Removal Act. It called for the forced relocation of all Native people east of the Mississippi River to land west of the Mississippi known as Indian Territory. Jackson wanted whites to take over good land that legally belonged to Native nations. This forced relocation began in 1838, and Alabama's Cherokees, Chickasaws, Creeks, Choctaws, and Seminoles were driven westward. It took two

## THE TRAIL OF TEARS

Theodore Pease Russell was 19 years old when the Indian Removal Act forced Native Americans onto what became called the Trail of Tears. Fifty years after the event, he recalled visiting Cherokee people camped along the way:

*As the Indians came in they were furnished rations by lodges, each lodge to receive so much corn, oats, and fodder, after which they camped at the place assigned them. They received no other rations; the hunters supplied meat out of the woods. Each morning when the Indians broke camp they were told how far they had to go and in what direction.*

*I saw groups of boys at play, but do not know what some of their games were. Some were pitching arrows, while some of the larger were shooting at a target on a tree with their bows. . . .*

*When I heard the laughter of the boys and girls, I could hardly realize I was in an Indian camp, among people who had been called savages.*

William W. Bibb led Alabama's first constitutional convention in 1819.

**WORD TO KNOW**

**constitution** *a written document that contains all the governing principles of a state or country*

years for thousands of Native people from the east to walk the hundreds of miles west on what came to be known as the Trail of Tears. Along the way, thousands died of hunger, exhaustion, and disease.

## STATEHOOD

Alabama became a separate U.S. territory in 1817. In order to become a state, Alabama needed a **constitution**. Its first constitutional convention was held in Huntsville in July 1819, and Alabama—because it had a constitution and government in place—qualified for statehood. It was admitted to the United States on December 14, 1819.

After Indians were forced to leave, Alabama's white population grew, reaching 128,000 by 1820. The steamboat *Harriet* chugged along the Alabama River from Mobile to Montgomery, opening up trade in central Alabama. This made life on the frontier easier for white settlers.

# Alabama: From Territory to Statehood

## (1817–1819)

This map shows the original Alabama territory and the area (in yellow) that became the state of Alabama in 1819.

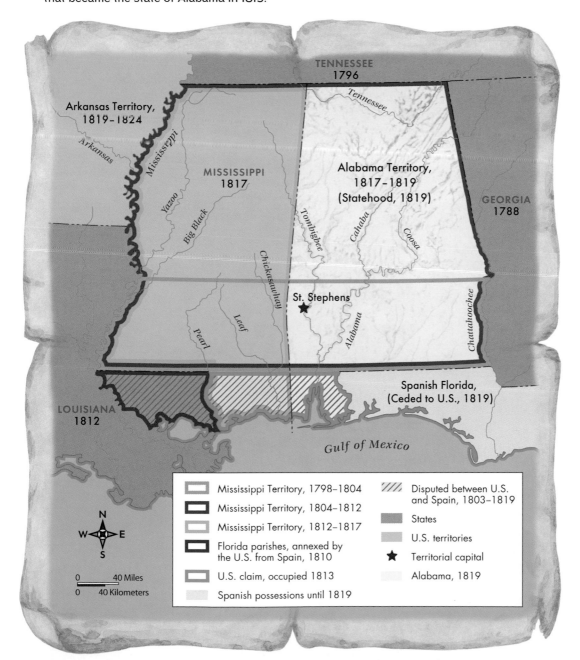

TENNESSEE
1796

Arkansas Territory,
1819–1824

*Tennessee*

*Arkansas*

*Mississippi*

Alabama Territory,
1817–1819
(Statehood, 1819)

GEORGIA
1788

MISSISSIPPI
1817

*Yazoo*

*Big Black*

*Tombigbee*

*Cahaba*

*Coosa*

*Chattahoochee*

*Chickasawhay*

★ St. Stephens

*Pearl*

*Leaf*

*Alabama*

LOUISIANA
1812

Spanish Florida,
(Ceded to U.S., 1819)

*Gulf of Mexico*

N
W—E
S

0    40 Miles
0    40 Kilometers

Legend:
- Mississippi Territory, 1798–1804
- Mississippi Territory, 1804–1812
- Mississippi Territory, 1812–1817
- Florida parishes, annexed by the U.S. from Spain, 1810
- U.S. claim, occupied 1813
- Spanish possessions until 1819
- /// Disputed between U.S. and Spain, 1803–1819
- States
- U.S. territories
- ★ Territorial capital
- Alabama, 1819

## as an Alabama Settler

If you are a girl in early Alabama, your days begin before sunup, stoking the fire and cooking breakfast. Before lunch, you must feed and water the animals, carry buckets of water for cooking and drinking from the nearby creek, and help with harvesting corn. Yesterday's hunt yielded a deer that must be skinned and butchered. That work is added to your normal chores of cleaning, cooking, doing laundry by hand, making soap and candles, sewing clothing, and skinning and drying fish.

Corn is the family's staple food, served at nearly every meal. Today's corn harvest must be husked and the corn dried. When the kernels are ready, you will spend hours scraping them from the cob, a tedious job that leaves your hands and back aching.

# FAQ

### Q: WHERE DID THE PHRASE "STARS FELL ON ALABAMA" COME FROM?

A: On the night of November 12–13, 1833, people saw a great meteor shower in Alabama. Some 8,000 meteors—often called shooting stars—appeared in less than half an hour. This was the Leonids shower, which occurred as Earth passed through the tail of comet Tempel-Tuttle. Meteors, the streaks of light in the sky, happen when tiny dust particles strike Earth's atmosphere at high speed. "Stars Fell on Alabama" now appears on the Alabama license plate.

Alabama was the frontier, and living on the frontier was hard work. Settlers arrived to find their land covered by forest. They needed to clear it of trees to create fields for crops. Families needed shelter, and most built log cabins.

## THE CIVIL WAR

As a presidential candidate, Abraham Lincoln had pledged to keep slavery from spreading westward. Some slaveholders saw his election in 1860 as a grave threat. "Fire-eaters" in the South pressed for the Confederacy, a group of states pledged to uphold slavery, even if it meant war. Pushing Alabama toward secession and war was Governor A. B. Moore. A week before the secession vote, he ordered Alabama troops to seize federal facilities such as Fort Gaines, Fort Morgan, and a U.S. weapons depot at Mount Vernon. When Alabama representatives approved secession from the Union by a vote of 61 to 39, most "no" votes came from northern counties, where slavery was less firmly established.

In 1861, when Alabama joined the Confederacy, most of its residents were poor whites, and 45 percent were enslaved African American men, women, and children. Few people in Alabama owned slaves, especially in northern Alabama. But a slaveholding minority owned huge plantations and thousands of people. The wealth produced gave them immense political power.

Montgomery became the capital of the new Confederacy. Jefferson Davis took his presidential oath of office on the steps of the state capitol. And Confederate troops from the 11 Confederate states, largely funded by a $500,000 loan from Alabama, marched out to battle the United States.

But support for the Confederacy and the war was far from unanimous in Alabama. Some 90,000 to 100,000 white men from Alabama served in the Confederate army. Another 2,700 white men and 5,000-plus African American men enlisted in the Union army. In northern Alabama, small farmers engaged in **guerrilla** actions against Confederate troops, and toward the end of the war Confederate army desertions rose sharply.

## SEE IT HERE!

### OLD ALABAMA TOWN

In Old Alabama Town, near Montgomery, you can find out what life was like in Alabama during the 1800s. Three blocks of historic houses show how rich and poor people lived when Alabama first became a state. Old Alabama Town features barns, a one-room schoolhouse, a church, and a cotton gin.

## WORD TO KNOW

**guerrilla** *a type of warfare that is fought by soldiers who are not sponsored by a recognized government*

**Confederate soldiers in Mobile**

## Q8 WHAT WAS THE "FREE STATE OF WINSTON"?

A8 In northern Alabama, few farmers owned slaves and very few agreed to support the Confederate cause. While Alabama was embroiled in war, 2,500 northern Alabamians met at Looney's Tavern, in Winston County. They passed a resolution stating that Alabama could not legally secede from the United States. Their resolution also declared that Winston County had ceased to be a part of Alabama and was, instead, the Free State of Winston.

African American soldiers and sailors were crucial to the Union victory in Alabama. During the battle of Mobile Bay in 1864, *Hartford* crewman John Lawson was wounded in the leg by a Confederate shell. Still, he kept the big guns firing, an act of courage that won him the Congressional Medal of Honor.

Black troops were among those who stormed Fort Blakely and captured Mobile in 1864. Nine black regiments of the 1st Union Division were crucial to the attack, suffering the heaviest casualties. Their white

**The battle of Mobile Bay began on August 5, 1864.**

commanding officer wrote that his men were "convincing proof that the former slaves of the South cannot be excelled as soldiers."

The Confederate war effort depended heavily on Alabama for supplies. The state provided corn and pork to the South's soldiers. Ten thousand civilians worked in the Confederate weapons and ammunition factories in Selma, Alabama. Women knitted socks, sewed uniforms, and rolled bandages to be sent to rebel troops. Enslaved workers brought in crops, as slave patrols increased.

## RECONSTRUCTION AND REFORM

The war ended in April 1865 when Confederate general Robert E. Lee surrendered. But Lieutenant General Richard Taylor, commander of the Department of Alabama, Mississippi, and East Louisiana, ordered his 12,000 Confederate soldiers to fight into May before he quit. Taylor's action was the first sign that slaveholders did not accept their defeat and the end of slavery. It made clear that more than roads, bridges, plantations, and homes needed to be rebuilt in the war-torn state. Congress demanded that the former slave states treat all citizens equally, including the 439,000 former slaves. But in Alabama, resistance to Congress marked the era known as Reconstruction.

Long denied an education and freed with little more than the clothes on their backs, former slaves started a new life. Many first searched for relatives who had been sold away during slavery. Then families had to find homes and jobs and learn to use their freedom.

## CIVIL WAR SUBMARINE

Built in Mobile with private funds, the Confederate submarine *H. L. Hunley* was powered by hand. Seven sailors turned the propeller, while an officer steered the boat. Shaped like a torpedo, the *Hunley* was 39.5 feet (12 m) long and weighed 7.5 tons. In 1864, off the coast of Charleston, South Carolina, it successfully torpedoed the U.S.S. *Housatonic*, which became the first warship sunk by submarine attack. Near that site, the *Hunley* itself sank. The wreck of the *Hunley* was discovered in 1970, but not raised from the bottom of Charleston Harbor until August 2000.

Want to know more? Check out *Secrets of a Civil War Submarine: Solving the Mysteries of the* H.L. Hunley by Sally M. Walker (Minneapolis: Carolrhoda Books, 2005)

Lt. General Richard Taylor, the man who surrendered Alabama to the Union, was the son of President Zachary Taylor, the 12th president of the United States.

56

## MINI-BIO

### JULIA STRUDWICK TUTWILER: EDUCATOR, REFORMER, WRITER

Julia Strudwick Tutwiler (1841–1916) devoted her life to education and prison reform. She was known as the mother of coeducation in Alabama after she forced the University of Alabama to accept its first ten female students. In the state's prisons, she worked to separate serious criminals from those who committed minor offenses, and she challenged harsh labor conditions for prisoners rented out to work in local mines. Alabama honored Tutwiler by selecting her for the Alabama Women's Hall of Fame in 1970.

**? Want to know more?** See www.awhf.org/tutwiler.html

A depiction of an Alabama village built by former slaves

The federal government set up a Freedmen's Bureau to feed hungry white and black people, and to be sure bosses did not exploit newly free workers. But resistance by former slaveholders to the bureau and any efforts to impose equality and justice for African Americans became massive and often violent.

By 1867, the U.S. Congress ordered new constitutional conventions in Alabama and the other Confederate states. U.S. troops stood by as male

An African American school in the early 1900s

citizens elected delegates of both races. Though black men accounted for 45 percent of voters, only 18 of the 100 delegates were African American.

White and black delegates created the state's first public school system. They established voting rights for men of all races, and ended discrimination based on color. Their constitution extended property rights for women. To protect poor people, it did away with imprisonment for debt.

Black people were pleased that their children were finally allowed to attend school. But white opposition kept education **segregated** for another century. The Ku Klux Klan (a white supremacist group) burned down many black schools.

**WORD TO KNOW**

**segregated** *separated from others, according to race, class, ethnic group, religion, or other factors*

## WORD TO KNOW

**sharecropping** *farming another person's land in exchange for a portion of the profits minus the landowner's cost for providing equipment and living quarters*

In Alabama, black people served as police officers, sheriffs, and other public officials. In 1873, a black Alabama convention urged the end of **sharecropping** and demanded written labor contracts, seeking to prevent bosses from cheating workers.

By July 1868, Alabama and six other states had been readmitted to the Union. Congress's plan for Reconstruction lasted less than six years. Racist politicians in Alabama and elsewhere in the South learned to play black people and their white allies against one another. Klan raiders then used intimidation and violence to keep black voters at home on election days. In 1874, Alabama's Reconstruction government was toppled by violence and election fraud. When the governor refused to help them, black men tried to organize their own state militia. They managed to elect 35 legislators, but freedom's days were numbered.

During Alabama's Reconstruction, the support of 20,000 or more white Republicans helped elect three black men to the U.S. Congress.

Born into slavery, Benjamin S. Turner went on to become a successful businessman and the first African American member of the U.S. Congress from Alabama.

As Alabama recovered from the Civil War, its economy became more industrialized, with steel and iron plants expanding in Birmingham. Cotton remained the primary agricultural product, but the 20th century and the arrival of destructive insects called boll weevils spelled even more changes for Alabamians.

A view of the capitol in the mid-1800s

**MINI-BIO**

## JAMES T. RAPIER: CONGRESSMAN

Born free and raised by his enslaved grandparents, James T. Rapier (1837–1883) was a statesman. He studied Greek and Latin and attended colleges in Canada, the United States, and Scotland. He became a wealthy cotton planter and in 1870 was nominated for Alabama secretary of state. He lost, through Klan violence. Rapier organized the Alabama Negro Labor Union and became its president. It denounced the harsh working conditions for sharecroppers and tenant farmers. In 1872, Rapier founded a newspaper and won a seat in Congress. As a representative, Rapier worked to increase education and curb violence in Alabama. In his bid for reelection in 1874, he was defeated by massive violence and intimidation. Still, 35 other black men were elected to the Alabama legislature.

**? Want to know more?** See http://alabamamoments.alabama.gov/sec24image.html

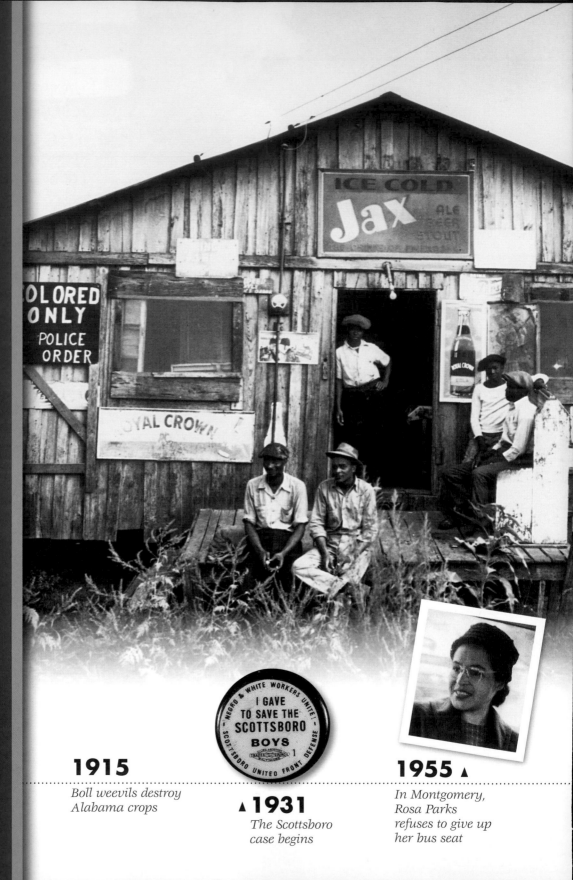

Throughout Alabama and the South, most blacks were required to shop at black-only stores such as this general store.

**1915**
*Boll weevils destroy Alabama crops*

▲**1931**
*The Scottsboro case begins*

I GAVE TO SAVE THE SCOTTSBORO BOYS
NEGRO & WHITE WORKERS UNITE!
SCOTTSBORO UNITED FRONT DEFENSE

**1955** ▲
*In Montgomery, Rosa Parks refuses to give up her bus seat*

CHAPTER FIVE

# MORE MODERN TIMES

★

**W**HEN RECONSTRUCTION ENDED, MANY WHITE ALABAMIANS WANTED TO GO BACK TO THE WAY THINGS HAD BEEN DURING SLAVERY. In 1896, the U.S. Supreme Court, in *Plessy v. Ferguson*, said states could provide "separate but equal" facilities for blacks. This allowed public schools, stores, movie theaters, and restrooms for whites to be kept separate from those for blacks.

**◄ 1965**
*Martin Luther King Jr. leads a protest march from Selma to Montgomery*

**◄ 1994**
*Ms. Alabama, Heather Whitestone, becomes the first Miss America with a disability*

**2003**
*Controversy erupts over the Ten Commandments display in the Alabama Judicial Building*

## UNFAIR LAWS

The policy of separate but equal was called segregation, and the laws that promoted it were called Jim Crow laws, named for a comic character. When Jim Crow laws were put in place, the freedoms gained by people of color at the end of the Civil War were lost.

Alabama landowners found in sharecropping a way to grow cotton with little or no risk. Sharecropping, or tenant farms, replaced slave labor and had added benefits for the landowner. A laborer rented land from the landowner. The landowner told his tenants what to grow (usually cotton or corn) and provided the seeds and tools. Sharecroppers gave half their crop back to the landowner and paid expenses for use of his land. Tenants rarely saw any profit from their crops. They just fell deeper into debt every year. But African Americans knew if they complained, they would face danger and violence.

Sharecroppers in a cotton field near Huntsville in 1906

By 1909, African Americans were burdened by debt, unfair laws, and poor education. Then a plague landed on Alabama's cotton farms: it was the boll weevil, a beetle that laid its eggs in cotton bolls, or pods. When the eggs hatched, the larvae ate the cotton from the inside out, destroying the crops. By 1915, boll weevils had eaten their way through Alabama's cotton crops, so there was no cotton to sell. But in Enterprise, Alabama, local farmers realized that because of the boll weevil, they had to vary their crops. The town wound up prospering and its citizens erected a statue honoring the boll weevil.

## THE GREAT MIGRATION

For recently freed African American Alabamians, the North beckoned as a promised land. Newspaper articles described how much better jobs and life were in New York, Philadelphia, and Chicago. Northern schools were

Many African American families left southern states such as Alabama and headed north to cities such as Chicago and New York.

A class poses for a portrait at the Tuskegee Institute in the 1890s.

better and often integrated, so African American children would be able to attend a school with adequate facilities. The movement of African Americans from the rural South to the urban North, called the Great Migration, began in the early 1900s and continued into the 1960s.

African Americans who chose to remain in Alabama sought ways to better their lives. African American colleges and universities—including the Tuskegee Institute, Alabama Agricultural and Mechanical University, and Alabama State University—provided courses in agriculture and technology. These schools educated African American doctors, teachers, lawyers, nurses, and scientists, as well as farmers and ministers.

## THE GREAT DEPRESSION

For years, cotton profits fell as hungry weevils ate the cotton plants. When the stock market crashed in October 1929, Alabama's economy was already in trouble. In Alabama, the Great Depression caused many people to lose their farms, businesses, and homes. Unemployment grew in rural and urban areas.

During the 1930s when jobs were scarce, many young people hopped aboard freight trains to search for work at different stops. This was illegal, but many still did it. In March 1931, aboard a freight train, nine African American youths aged 13 to 21 got into a fight with some white boys on the train. At Scottsboro, Alabama, lawmen arrested the nine blacks. Two white women were also arrested. Fearful of being jailed, the women accused the African American youths of assault. There was no evidence. The nine had no attorneys, and in four trials in four days, white juries convicted the "Scottsboro Boys." All but the youngest were sentenced to death.

In the North, political radicals, who held views that were extremely different from mainstream policies, began to publicize the case as a "legal **lynching**." People in dozens of cities protested the death sentences and demanded freedom for the nine. Twice the Scottsboro case came before the U.S. Supreme Court, and twice the Court reversed Alabama's convictions. But white Alabama juries continued to hand down guilty verdicts. Finally, one of the accusers, Ruby Bates, admitted the assault story was a lie. She joined the worldwide campaign to free the nine. None of the "Scottsboro Boys" was executed, but five had to spend years in jail. By the time they were all released, the Scottsboro case had focused world attention on racial injustice.

Meanwhile, the Depression followed a downward spiral, with unemployment and lost savings. Many people of all races were homeless; others had to stand in lines to get lukewarm soup and bread.

Scottsboro Boys Defense Fund pin

## WORD TO KNOW

**lynching** *to kill by mob without a lawful trial*

## UNION STRUGGLE

As the Scottsboro case wound through the courts, white radicals in Birmingham, Alabama, helped African Americans in Tallapoosa County organize a black farmworkers union. Twice in July 1931, when union members met with Max Coad, their organizer, they were attacked by a sheriff and his deputies. Five union members died and the sheriff was seriously wounded.

## THE TUSKEGEE AIRMEN

During World War II, African Americans enlisted in all branches of the military. But they were not allowed to be officers or serve in white regiments. The U.S. military was segregated. One group of potential black pilots gathered at Tuskegee Institute in Alabama for training. In 1941, these pilots entertained an honored guest, First Lady Eleanor Roosevelt. She went for a flight, with Charles "Chief" Anderson as her pilot. During the war, the Tuskegee Airmen flew 15,500 missions and earned Silver Stars, Purple Hearts, Distinguished Flying Crosses, the French Croix de Guerre, and the Yugoslavian Red Star. They proved that courage was not segregated.

Then Franklin Roosevelt became president. His New Deal created federal agencies to help promote economic recovery. Governments hired people to build libraries, roads, and schools in Alabama. The Tennessee Valley Authority (TVA) hired workers in many states to build dams along the river and develop hydroelectric plants to provide electricity.

But it was World War II in 1939 in Europe that pulled the country out of the Great Depression. Alabama's steel and iron factories went into full swing as Americans created war materials that were sold to its allies. In 1941, the United States entered the war. Then, men joined the military and women worked in the factories. The state produced cotton for uniforms, food for soldiers and sailors, and metal to build weapons and ammunition.

## THE CIVIL RIGHTS MOVEMENT

When African American soldiers returned to Alabama after World War II, they faced the same prejudices they had left. Black men had fought and died for their country. Black women had served as nurses, drivers,

Tuskegee Airmen read a map during a training exercise.

and factory employees. And yet, African Americans still could not sit in the front of a bus, eat in a "whites only" restaurant, or enter a library in Alabama.

African Americans were determined to achieve equality. On December 1, 1955, a soft-spoken seamstress named Rosa Parks got on a city bus. Parks was an activist who wanted to strike a blow for human rights and dignity. She sat down in the front of the bus and refused to move when ordered to by the bus driver. He called the police, and Rosa Parks was arrested.

Montgomery's black population, led by Martin Luther King Jr., supported Rosa Parks. They boycotted, or refused to use, the bus system for months. They walked to their jobs. Some organized car

**MINI-BIO**

## ROSA MCCAULEY PARKS: CIVIL RIGHTS PIONEER

Born in Tuskegee, Rosa McCauley Parks (1913–2005) joined the NAACP (National Association for the Advancement of Colored People) as a young woman. She wanted to improve the lives of segregated African Americans. A gentle, committed fighter, she said, "I worked on numerous cases with the NAACP, but we did not get the publicity. . . . It was more a matter of trying to challenge the powers that be, and to let it be known that we did not wish to continue being second-class citizens." Her refusal to leave her seat on a Montgomery bus led to a boycott of the bus company and eventually to active protests and positive changes across the South. Parks received a Congressional Gold Medal for her accomplishments in 1999.

**? Want to know more?** See www.rosaparks.org

## FROM "LETTER FROM BIRMINGHAM JAIL," APRIL 1963

Martin Luther King Jr. was a new minister at the Dexter Avenue Baptist Church in Montgomery when Rosa Parks was arrested in 1955. He agreed to lead African Americans in their fight for civil rights and equality. In 1963, he was arrested in Birmingham, Alabama, for parading without a permit. In jail, he wrote about the importance of liberty.

*Oppressed people cannot remain oppressed forever. The yearning for freedom eventually manifests itself, and that is what has happened to the American Negro. Something within has reminded him of his birthright of freedom, and something without has reminded him that it can be gained.*

At this point, President Lyndon Johnson realized he had to act. He sent troops and FBI agents to protect the marchers. On March 21, King led 25,000 protesters on a four-day march from Selma all the way to the capitol in Montgomery. There they handed a petition to Governor Wallace, demanding equal voting rights. Then President Johnson signed the Voting Rights Act on August 6, 1965, which outlawed restrictions on voting.

Civil rights came to Alabama's African Americans very slowly. But as voting by blacks increased, the number of blacks running for and being elected to office rose. In 1980, Oscar W. Adams Jr. became the first African American to serve on the Alabama Supreme Court. Judge Adams ran for and won reelection in 1982 and 1988.

## HARDSHIPS AND SUCCESSES

The state of Alabama has sometimes experienced hard times in recent decades. On May 15, 1972, while campaigning for the Democratic nomination for president, Governor Wallace was the victim of an attempted assassination, which left him paralyzed from the waist down.

Then, in 1993, Governor Guy Hunt, in his second term as the first Republican governor of the state since Reconstruction, was convicted of misuse of public funds and removed from office.

The Alabama Supreme Court found itself in the national news when, in 2003, Justice Roy S. Moore refused to obey a federal order to remove a display of the Ten Commandments from the Alabama Judicial Building. For this act, Moore was removed from office by the state's judicial ethics panel.

But Alabama has had plenty of high points, too. In 1994, Ms. Alabama, Heather Whitestone, became Miss

Visitors at the Civil Rights Memorial Center in Montgomery

America. Classified as deaf, Whitestone became the first contestant with a disability to win the pageant. She went on to promote awareness for people with disabilities.

## LOOKING TOWARD THE FUTURE

Alabamians have endured and overcome many challenges and hardships, including slavery, the Civil War, the Great Depression, and the struggle for civil rights for all its citizens. But the state has worked hard to improve the lives of its people. Today, Alabamians want their state to be a place of opportunity for all citizens.

# READ ABOUT

The Auburn Tigers marching band plays at a football game at Jordan-Hare Stadium in Auburn.

CHAPTER SIX

# PEOPLE

★

**M**ORE ALABAMIANS LIVE IN CITIES AND SUBURBS THAN IN THE COUNTRY. But Alabama's cities are not vast metropolitan areas like Los Angeles, Chicago, or New York City. They are closer to sprawling "small towns." Birmingham, with about 230,000 residents, is Alabama's largest city, followed by Montgomery, Mobile, and Huntsville.

# People QuickFacts

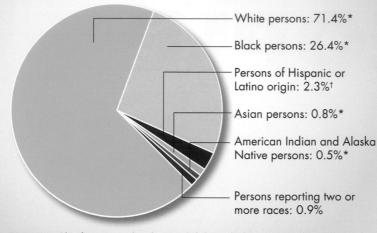

White persons: 71.4%*

Black persons: 26.4%*

Persons of Hispanic or Latino origin: 2.3%†

Asian persons: 0.8%*

American Indian and Alaska Native persons: 0.5%*

Persons reporting two or more races: 0.9%

*Hispanics may be of any race, so they also are included in applicable race categories
†Includes persons reporting only one race
Source: U.S. Census Bureau, 2005

## GETTING TO KNOW ALABAMIANS

The majority of Alabama's population is white, and just over a quarter is African American. Less than 1 percent of the population is Native American, mostly Creek or Cherokee. In the past 50 years, a growing number of Asian and Latino citizens have moved into Alabama's cities. But their total is still only about 3 percent of the population.

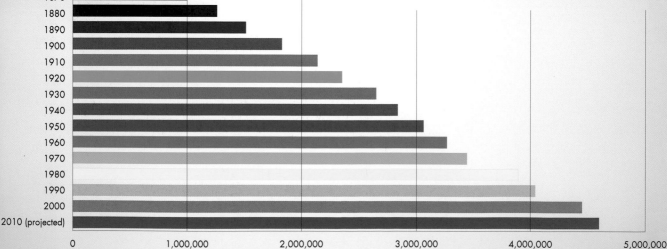

# Alabama Population Growth

This chart shows Alabama's population growth between 1800 and 2000, and it projects that by 2010 there will be more than 4.5 million people living in the state.

Source: U.S. Census Bureau

## ARTS IN ALABAMA

Traditional arts and crafts in Alabama take many forms. Indian baskets, woven from natural cane or reeds, are still produced today. With the state's ties to cotton, it is not surprising that artisan weavers create rich, eye-catching fabrics. Remarkable hand-stitched quilts have been made for over a century by African American women in rural Gees Bend. Created from whatever scraps of fabric were at hand, these quilts tell a powerful story of determination, struggle, and survival.

Potter Jerry Brown represents the ninth generation in a family of pottery makers. His traditional pottery is made and decorated by hand. And all his clay is ground and mixed in a mule-driven mill. His mule, Blue, is harnessed to the mill and powers the machine by walking in a circle.

## MUSIC

Gospel singing, religious singing that originated in the South in the late 19th century, and **shape-note singing** are heard in churches, at family reunions, and in concert halls. Over the radio and in person, the Gandy Dancers recall the chants and calls that allowed Alabama's railroad workers to time their work. The Wiregrass Sacred Harp Singers lift their voices in traditional hymns and songs of praise or prayer such as "Coronation" and "New Jordan."

The blues, a type of music that traces its origins to African American spirituals, was introduced to the rest of America by Alabama native W. C. Handy, called the Father of the Blues. Songs in the blues tradition often have music and lyrics that repeat frequently and describe a troubled mood. Handy's hometown of Florence holds

### ALABAMA CAJUNS

About 4,500 people in rural southern Alabama call themselves Cajuns. They are not like the Cajuns of Louisiana, who have a French Acadian heritage. Alabama Cajuns are a mixture of several races, possibly including European, African, and Native American. The Cajuns represent a kinship group that has formed a unique ethnic community. No one knows why they call themselves Cajuns, but they prefer to remain isolated from other Alabamians.

**Quilter Mary Lee Bendolph of Gees Bend**

### WORD TO KNOW

**shape-note singing** *a tradition of church singing using hymns written with shaped notes, so singers don't have to be able to read music to participate; usually done without instrument accompaniment*

# Where Alabamians Live

The colors on this map indicate population density throughout the state. The darker the color, the more people live there.

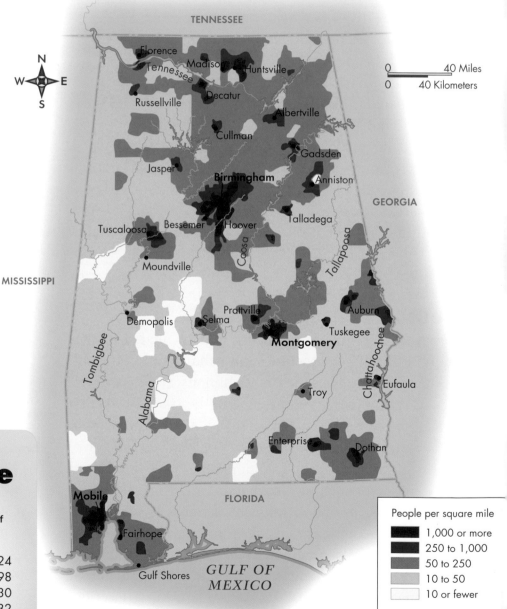

# Big City Life

This list shows the population of Alabama's biggest cities.

**Birmingham** . . . . . . . .229,424
**Montgomery** . . . . . . .201,998
**Mobile** . . . . . . . . . . .192,830
**Huntsville** . . . . . . . . .168,132
**Tuscaloosa** . . . . . . . . .83,052
**Hoover** . . . . . . . . . . . .68,707

Source: U.S. Census Bureau, 2006 estimates

People per square mile

- 1,000 or more
- 250 to 1,000
- 50 to 250
- 10 to 50
- 10 or fewer

**MINI-BIO**

### W. C. HANDY: BRINGING HOME THE BLUES

The son of a preacher, William Christopher "W. C." Handy (1873–1958) was born in Florence, Alabama, with music in his soul. As a young man, he studied and eventually taught music at Huntsville College. He first heard the blues while traveling through rural Mississippi. Drawn to this sound, Handy began composing blues music. By publishing his compositions, he brought blues music to the world. His "St. Louis Blues" is one of the most widely recorded blues songs. Handy's autobiography bears the title Father of the Blues, and no title could be more appropriate.

**? Want to know more?** See www2.una.edu/library/handy

**WOW**

Two Alabamians have won on the popular television show *American Idol*: Taylor Hicks and Reuben Studdard, both from Birmingham.

the W. C. Handy Music Festival every summer, featuring musicians such as The Commodores, Percy Sledge, the Alabama Blues Brothers, and dozens of others.

In Arab, the Long Branch Opry frequently hosts bluegrass musicians. There, fans listen to this guitar-strummin', banjo-pickin', fabulous-fiddlin', down-home country music.

Rock, jazz, and country-and-western artists also follow the musical traditions of Alabama. Alabamians Lionel Ritchie, Emmy Lou Harris, and Taylor Hicks, as well as the group Alabama have topped the charts in the pop and country categories.

Taylor Hicks

## HOW TO TALK LIKE AN ALABAMIAN

Alabamians, like most Americans, have some interesting terms for common items. Here are just a few:

| Alabamian Phrase | Common Term |
| --- | --- |
| Snake doctor, snake feeder, or mosquito hawk | Dragonfly |
| Harp | Harmonica |
| Tow sack or croker sack | Burlap bag |
| Y'all | You all |
| Gopher | Burrowing turtle |

## HOW TO EAT LIKE AN ALABAMIAN

Alabama tables brim with southern traditional "comfort" foods, like fried chicken and mashed potatoes for dinner, and pecan pie for dessert. But you'll also find fresh fruits and vegetables from Alabama farms, like satsuma oranges and string beans. Southern cooking blends multiple traditions, from African American influences, such as hearty greens and sweet potatoes, to rural influences, such as cornbread and grits.

Fried chicken

# MENU

## WHAT'S ON THE MENU IN ALABAMA?

★ ★ ★

### Grits

Grits are coarsely ground hulled grain, especially hominy (corn). Hot grits are served for breakfast, topped with butter, but they can also be a tasty side dish with shrimp or fish.

### Turnip greens

Turnip greens are cooked until limp, flavored with pepper vinegar.

### Cornbread

Cornbread is a traditional American food, found in nearly every region of the country. In the South, a basket of cornbread on the table makes any meal complete.

### Fried green tomatoes

Thick slices of tomatoes are salted and peppered, dipped in milk, then breaded with cornmeal. Finally, they are sautéed in olive oil until golden brown on both sides.

### Satsumas

Never heard of a satsuma? It is a type of orange native to Alabama—and it's delicious.

### TRY THIS RECIPE
### Sweet Potato Pie

Sweet potatoes are delicious and packed with nutrition. A familiar side dish at Thanksgiving, sweet potatoes can also be baked into breads, muffins, and pies.

**Ingredients:**
1 box vanilla wafers
4 large sweet potatoes,
   peeled, boiled until soft, and mashed
2 cups sugar
1 stick butter or margarine, softened
½ tsp. cinnamon
¼ tsp. nutmeg
2 eggs, lightly beaten
½ cup evaporated milk

**Instructions:**
Preheat oven to 350°F.
Coat a pie pan with nonstick spray and line with vanilla wafers. Put the remaining ingredients in a mixing bowl and blend until smooth. Pour the mixture into the pie pan. Bake 35-40 minutes, or until a toothpick inserted in the center comes out clean.

Sweet potato pie

Fried green tomatoes

**MINI-BIO**

## HENRY LOUIS "HANK" AARON: HOME-RUN KING

He was born in Mobile and baseball was his claim to fame. Henry Louis "Hank" Aaron (1934–) started his career playing amateur and semipro ball, including a stint with the Indianapolis Clowns of the Negro American League. In 1954, the Milwaukee Braves (now the Atlanta Braves) offered Aaron a contract. Aaron beat Babe Ruth's long-standing home-run record with his 715th homer. By the time he retired, he had reached a record 755 homers. Aaron was inducted into the National Baseball Hall of Fame in 1982.

**? Want to know more?** See www.baseballhalloffame.org/hofers_and_honorees/hofer_bios/aaron_hank.htm

## ALABAMA SPORTS

Sporting events attract plenty of attention, from youngsters playing T-ball to professional teams in the big cities. NASCAR events draw Alabamians from all over the state to the Talladega Superspeedway. The speedway stands accommodate 143,000 fans, with room for thousands more on the racetrack infield.

NASCAR driver Bobby LaBonte makes a pit stop during a race at the Talladega Superspeedway.

Several Alabama cities support professional sports teams. Birmingham, Huntsville, and Mobile are home to AA minor-league baseball teams. Mobile's BayBears have a lot to live up to, since they play in the stadium named for the legendary Henry "Hammerin' Hank" Aaron. This may be the South, but ice hockey is making inroads as Mobile's Mysticks and Birmingham's Bulls send slap shots toward the goal. Football in Alabama means Friday night high school games and Saturday afternoon college games. The University of Alabama's Crimson Tide and Auburn's Tigers have a long-lived rivalry that has fans either roaring in the stadium or glued to their television sets.

Whether they live in big cities or small towns, apartment buildings or farmhouses, the people of Alabama have much to brag about. Their state has produced astronauts and teachers, athletes and musicians, artists and writers, and activists and leaders, all of whom have contributed greatly to American culture.

# WOW

NASCAR legend Bobby Allison won 84 races. He made Alabama his home and was a member of a group of drivers called the Alabama Gang.

## MINI-BIO

## MIA HAMM-GARCIAPARRA: ON THE BALL

Soccer star Mia Hamm-Garciaparra (1972–) was born in Selma. Before retiring at the end of 2004, she scored a record 149 goals in international play. Hamm was on the U.S. team that took two wins in the Women's World Cup and won an Olympic gold medal in the Athens Olympics of 2004. Many consider her the best female soccer player in the world.

She has created the Mia Hamm Foundation to support two causes that are important to her: bone marrow research (in honor of her brother who died from a bone marrow disease) and the encouragement of young female athletes.

**? Want to know more?** See www.miafoundation.org

## READ ABOUT

Members of Alabama's Boys and Girls State program met with Governor Don Siegelman in 2002, during a summer event to learn about state government.

CHAPTER SEVEN

# GOVERNMENT

★

ALABAMA'S ELECTIONS BRING OUT POLITICIANS FROM EVERY WALK OF LIFE. Hopeful candidates attend supermarket openings, high school football games, church socials, and blood drives. They also set up Web sites, place ads on TV, and participate in debates and radio talk shows. These men and women want to get to know the people they hope to represent. That knowledge would help them make good decisions for Alabamians.

## CONSTITUTIONS AND CAPITALS

Alabama has had six constitutions and five capitals. Compared to most states, that's a good deal of change, but the changes came about for good reasons.

The state's first constitution was written and approved (ratified) in 1819 as part of Alabama's bid for statehood. Forty-two years later, Alabama seceded from the Union to join the Confederate States of America, and a new constitution noted the change.

The loss of the Civil War brought about two new constitutions: one in 1865 (ending the connection to the Confederacy) and another in 1868 (reflecting Reconstruction). Additional constitutions in 1875 and 1901 changed minor items, but all set up the state government into three branches. The responsibilities of government to its citizens and the rights of citizens living in Alabama are also listed.

The Alabama state capitol sits on Goat Hill in Montgomery.

Beginning with its status as a territory in 1817, Alabama chose and changed the seat of state government several times. The U.S. Congress chose the first capital, Saint Stephens, in southwest Alabama. Alabamians did not like the location and changed it to Cahaba, a more centrally located city. The second session of the Alabama legislature met in Cahaba.

## CAPITOL FACTS

Here are some interesting facts about Alabama's state capitol. In 1846, Andrew Dexter, one of Montgomery's founders, selected an ideal site for the state's new capitol—Goat Hill, Montgomery. At that time, the land served as a pasture. The state issued $75,000 in **bonds** to pay for buying the land and building the capitol, which was completed in December 1847. In 1849, the first capitol burned and had to be replaced. The new building, designed by architect Barachias Holt, was built on top of the existing foundation from the first capitol and features tall columns and a central dome. On this new capitol's steps, Jefferson Davis took the oath of office and became the first and only president of the Confederate States of America.

# Capital City

This map shows places of interest in Montgomery, Alabama's capital city.

## WORD TO KNOW

**bonds** *interest-bearing loan agreements made to raise specific amounts of money in a specified period of time*

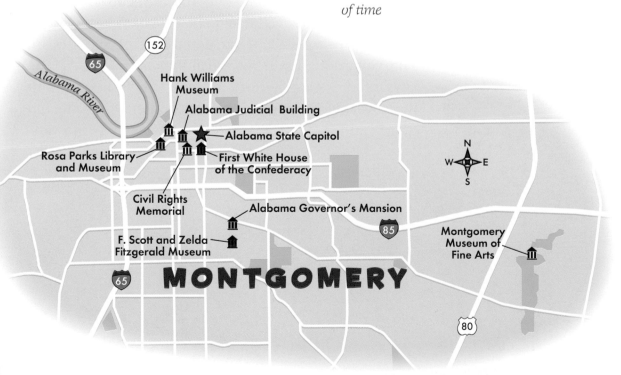

## FAQ

### Q: WHERE DOES THE GOVERNOR LIVE?

**A:** The official home of Alabama's governor is the governor's mansion. Built in 1907 as the home of General Robert Ligon, the mansion is fronted by columns and has a formal garden surrounded by a high wall. The state bought the home in 1950 and later added a swimming pool shaped like Alabama.

Governor Bob Riley addresses a U.S. Senate committee in Washington, D.C., in 2006.

The 1825–1826 legislatures decided that Cahaba flooded too easily. Tuscaloosa, a prospering community on the Black Warrior River, became the new capital in 1826. As the state grew, it became obvious that Tuscaloosa, in the western part of the state, was an inconvenient choice. In 1846, the legislature decided that Montgomery was centrally located and easily reached, and it has been the state capital ever since.

## THE EXECUTIVE BRANCH

When most people hear the word "executive" referring to a state, they think "governor." While the governor is the chief executive of the state, the executive branch is much larger than just one person. Like the cabinet of the president of the United States, there are several department heads who offer advice to the governor on everything from agriculture and banking to public safety and children's affairs. More than two dozen departments report to the governor and help run the state. To date, 52 people have served as Alabama's governor.

Alabama's governor is elected to a four-year term. The governor's main responsibility is to execute the laws of the state. Enforcing laws costs money, and the governor must plan how state money is collected (taxes) and spent. Alabama's state budget covers a varietv of expenses, including building roads and schools, providing health care for the needy, encouraging tourism, supporting the unemployed, and maintaining state police. Every function of state government that requires money—and most do—is listed in the budget.

## THE LEGISLATIVE BRANCH

The legislative branch in Alabama mirrors the legislature of the U.S. government. There is a house of representatives and a senate. Each has its function in creating and passing state laws.

The 105 members of the house of representatives speak for districts of roughly 40,000 people. Terms of office in the house last four years. Alabama wants its representatives to be close to their people and requires that representatives live in their districts. The person in charge of house meetings is the Speaker of the House. Elected by the membership, the Speaker usually belongs to the political party in power.

The Alabama senate is about one-third the size of the house of representatives. Each senator represents about 130,000 Alabamians. Senators must be 25 years old when elected and have lived in their districts for one year and in Alabama for three years. They, too, are elected to four-year terms.

In Alabama, the house of representatives can introduce potential laws that deal with revenue (money), but those bills can be revised or rejected by the senate. The senate also confirms officials appointed by the governor. The appointee goes before a senate hearing, after which he or she is recommended or rejected.

The state lieutenant governor serves as president of the senate, though the only time the lieutenant governor can vote in the senate is to break a tie vote.

**Members of the Alabama house of representatives are paid only $10 per day for their services, plus travel expenses.**

# Alabama State Government

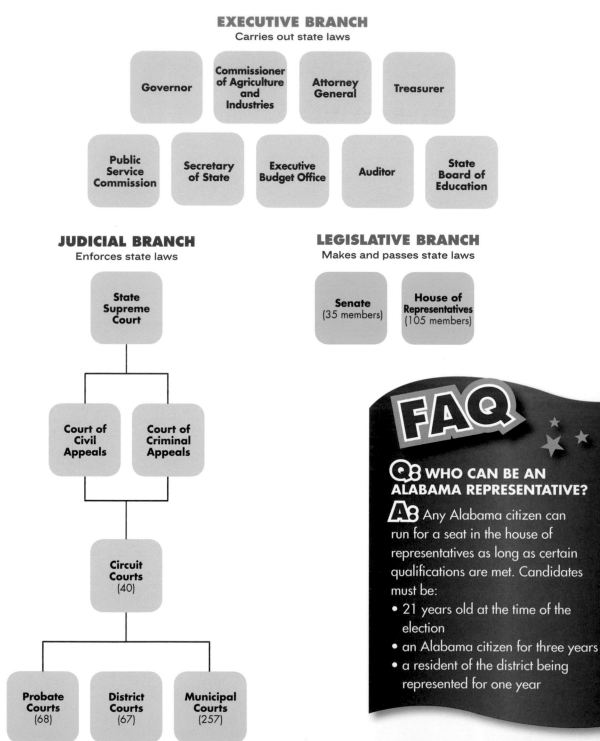

## EXECUTIVE BRANCH
Carries out state laws

- Governor
- Commissioner of Agriculture and Industries
- Attorney General
- Treasurer
- Public Service Commission
- Secretary of State
- Executive Budget Office
- Auditor
- State Board of Education

## JUDICIAL BRANCH
Enforces state laws

- State Supreme Court
  - Court of Civil Appeals
  - Court of Criminal Appeals
  - Circuit Courts (40)
    - Probate Courts (68)
    - District Courts (67)
    - Municipal Courts (257)

## LEGISLATIVE BRANCH
Makes and passes state laws

- Senate (35 members)
- House of Representatives (105 members)

## FAQ

**Q8 WHO CAN BE AN ALABAMA REPRESENTATIVE?**

**A8** Any Alabama citizen can run for a seat in the house of representatives as long as certain qualifications are met. Candidates must be:

- 21 years old at the time of the election
- an Alabama citizen for three years
- a resident of the district being represented for one year

## THE JUDICIAL BRANCH

Alabama's judicial branch makes sure that laws passed by the legislature and enforced by the executive branch do not violate the state constitution. The Judicial

The Alabama Court of the Judiciary in session at the Supreme Court chamber in Montgomery

MINI-BIO

## CONDOLEEZZA RICE: SECRETARY OF STATE

When she was a child in Montgomery, Condoleezza Rice (1954–) lost a friend in the 1963 bombing of the Sixteenth Street Baptist Church. And growing up during segregation made her aware that African American children had to be "twice as good as white kids to stay even—and three times as good to get ahead." Her parents always encouraged her to work hard and do her best, making her feel she could be president if she wanted to be.

Confident and focused, Rice followed her interests throughout school. She went on to earn a doctorate in political science, and she became a professor at Stanford University. In 2001, she was appointed national security adviser to President George W. Bush. In 2005, she became secretary of state, a position in which her determination and intelligence serve her well.

In 2004 and 2005, Rice was named the most powerful woman in the world by *Forbes* magazine.

**❓ Want to know more?** See www.whitehouse.gov/government/rice-bio.html

Building in Montgomery houses Alabama's three highest courts: the supreme court, the court of civil appeals, and the court of criminal appeals.

State law requires all judges to be trained, licensed lawyers. Judges preside over the lower courts, and justices sit in the higher courts. Regardless of where they work, judges and justices must run for election. High court justices are elected statewide. Lower court judges run in the district where they serve. If a vacancy occurs in a court judgeship, a temporary judge or justice can be appointed by the governor or local governing body, depending on where the vacancy occurs, for the remaining time in the six-year term.

Laws apply to children just as they do adults. When children commit crimes, they are tried in the juvenile courts, which the judicial branch oversees. The rules of the juvenile courts are different, and guilty offenders face different punishments

# Representing Alabama

This list shows the number of elected officials who represent Alabama, both on the state and national levels.

| OFFICE | NUMBER | LENGTH OF TERM |
| --- | --- | --- |
| **State representatives** | 105 | 4 years |
| **State senators** | 35 | 4 years |
| **U.S. representatives** | 9 | 2 years |
| **U.S. senators** | 2 | 6 years |
| **Presidential electors** | 9 | — |

# Alabama Counties

This map shows the 67 counties in Alabama. Montgomery, the state capital, is indicated with a star.

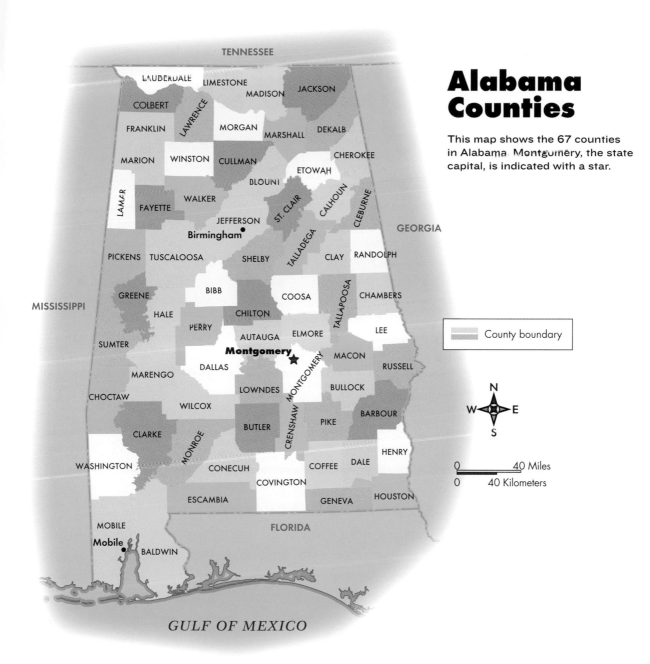

TENNESSEE

LAUDERDALE
LIMESTONE
MADISON
JACKSON
COLBERT
FRANKLIN
LAWRENCE
MORGAN
MARSHALL
DEKALB
MARION
WINSTON
CULLMAN
CHEROKEE
ETOWAH
BLOUNT
LAMAR
WALKER
ST. CLAIR
CALHOUN
CLEBURNE
FAYETTE
JEFFERSON
Birmingham
TALLADEGA
PICKENS
TUSCALOOSA
SHELBY
CLAY
RANDOLPH
GREENE
BIBB
COOSA
CHAMBERS
HALE
CHILTON
TALLAPOOSA
PERRY
ELMORE
LEE
AUTAUGA
SUMTER
Montgomery
DALLAS
MACON
RUSSELL
MARENGO
LOWNDES
MONTGOMERY
BULLOCK
CHOCTAW
WILCOX
CRENSHAW
BARBOUR
CLARKE
BUTLER
PIKE
MONROE
HENRY
WASHINGTON
CONECUH
COFFEE
DALE
COVINGTON
ESCAMBIA
GENEVA
HOUSTON
MOBILE
FLORIDA
Mobile
BALDWIN

MISSISSIPPI

GEORGIA

County boundary

N W E S

0        40 Miles
0    40 Kilometers

GULF OF MEXICO

than do adults. They may be sent to a children's **correctional** facility, where they eat, sleep, and attend school. They may be put on probation, which allows the child to live at home with regular checks by court officials.

**THINK ABOUT IT!**

# Seat Belts on School Buses?

## PRO

Some people wonder why most school buses do not have seat belts like other vehicles do. They believe that there is no good argument for not equipping school buses with seat belts. Senator Steve French thinks it makes sense to require seat belts. He says, "There is virtually no other form of transportation where seat belts are not required."

## CON

The National Highway Traffic Safety Association says that buses are designed in a special way. This makes them safer than other vehicles. Also, adding seat belts to buses would be expensive. And waiting for students to buckle up would make the bus route take longer. According to Michael Sibley, an Alabama state Department of Education spokesman, "We subscribe to the fact that school buses . . . are a very safe mode of transportation for children. It's the safest mode of transportation to and from schools."

## EDUCATION EFFORTS

Funding education is a large part of the state's budget. The executive and legislative branches both suggest ways to help keep Alabama's schools safe and successful with a focus on student achievement, quality teachers, a challenging curriculum, and effective administrators.

To improve students' reading, math, and science skills, the state has begun programs promoting those areas. One example is AMSTI (Alabama Math, Science, and Technology Initiative), which is designed to help improve math and science teaching statewide. The governor championed the program in 2005, and the

Alabama legislature provided $15 million from the state's budget to fund it in 2006; funding was increased to $22 million in 2007. Other education programs funded by the state include the Alabama Reading Initiative (ARI) and Alabama Connecting Classrooms, Educators, and Students Statewide (ACCESS). ARI, a program that earned a national award, furthers reading skills in 752 Alabama schools. ACCESS offers distance learning to high school students.

The emphasis on education is working. In recent years, record numbers of Alabama students—more than three-fourths of eligible students—took the American College Test (ACT). In addition, Scholastic Aptitude Test (SAT) scores have exceeded the national averages for the past 14 years.

## KEEPING KIDS SAFE

Alabama has passed several laws with children in mind. Until recently, only children under six years old had to wear seat belts in cars (drivers and passengers in the front seat also had to wear seat belts). In 2006, the Child Passenger and Safety Legislation went into effect. This law requires all children 15 and under to be in appropriate restraints while riding in the rear seats of vehicles that carry 10 passengers or fewer. Another child-related law is the Brad Hudson Alabama Bicycle Safety Act of 1995. This law requires all bike riders to wear safety helmets, follow traffic laws, and use a restraining seat for carrying young passengers.

In Alabama, all bike riders must wear helmets.

# State Flag

For many years, Alabama was without a flag. But on February 16, 1895—76 years after first being admitted to the Union—the Alabama legislature authorized the crimson cross of St. Andrew on a field of white as its official flag. This type of cross bears St. Andrew's name because, according to tradition, he was crucified on a cross of this shape. It is also known as a saltire cross. Alabama's flag is sometimes square and at other times rectangular.

# State Seal

The Alabama senate and house approved the Great Seal of Alabama in 1939. In the outer circle, the words *Alabama Great Seal* are prominently displayed. The inner circle of the seal features an outline of the state of Alabama showing the state's major rivers, as well as the bordering states.

**READ ABOUT**

Farmers check on
their cotton crop.

CHAPTER EIGHT

# ECONOMY

★

EVER SINCE ALABAMA'S EARLIEST INHABITANTS CLEARED THE LAND AND PLANTED CROPS, AGRICULTURE HAS BEEN AN IMPORTANT PART OF ALABAMA'S ECONOMY. It has provided food to eat and crops to trade. By the 1800s, Alabama had a highly profitable cotton-based economy. But by planting cotton year after year, farmers overused the soil, damaging its structure and depleting its nutrients. In the early 1900s, disaster struck when a cotton-devouring boll weevil ruined the crop, causing Alabama's economy to hit rock bottom.

## GEORGE WASHINGTON CARVER: AN INVENTIVE MIND

In 1896, scientist George Washington Carver (1864–1943) became director of research at Tuskegee Normal and Industrial Institute. Carver saw that Alabama farmers needed new markets for their products. He experimented in his laboratory until he developed 300 products from peanuts and 118 products from sweet potatoes. We're not talking peanut butter here; he created adhesives, axle grease, bleach, buttermilk, ink, instant coffee, mayonnaise, talcum powder, wood stain, and shoe polish from those foods. He also was able to create synthetic marble from wood pulp.

Carver also introduced a method of crop rotation, a plan that changed Alabama farming forever. He taught farmers that planting soybeans, peas, peanuts, and sweet potatoes would enrich soil damaged by growing cotton. In 1943, the United States honored Carver with a national monument. When he died, he was one of the nation's most respected scientists.

**? Want to know more?** See www.nps.gov/gwca/

## BEYOND COTTON

Cotton takes valuable nutrients from its soil. Scientists discovered that planting soybeans, peas, peanuts, and sweet potatoes enriched soil that had been damaged by growing cotton. This practice, called crop rotation, changed Alabama farming forever. By rotating crops and applying fertilizer, farmers keep the soil healthy.

Alabama is still a strong farming state, but cotton is not the only, or even the major, product in the state. It ranks behind chickens, cattle, eggs, and plant nursery products in the top five of Alabama's farm products. Alabama rates nationally in production of farmed catfish, peanuts, sweet potatoes, and Irish spring potatoes, as well as broilers (young small chickens), of which Alabama sells more than 1 billion yearly.

Although large farms may make significant money, most Alabama farms are small and struggling. Fifty-three percent of farms are 1 to 99 acres (0.4 to 40 ha) in size; 60 percent sell less than $10,000 worth of products a year.

## NATURAL RESOURCES

Natural resources provide products for sale and employment for thousands of Alabamians. The state's forests include 23 million acres (9.3 million ha) of commercial

# Major Agricultural and Mining Products

This map shows where Alabama's major agricultural and mining products come from. See a salt shaker? That means salt is found there.

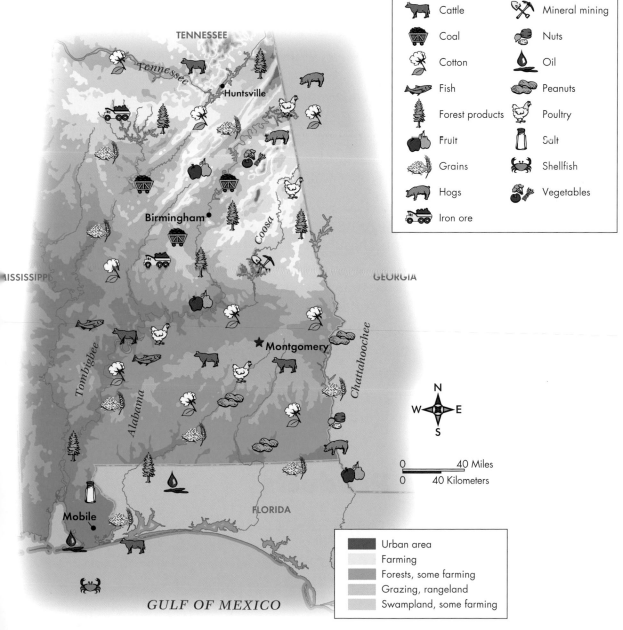

**Legend:**

- Cattle
- Coal
- Cotton
- Fish
- Forest products
- Fruit
- Grains
- Hogs
- Iron ore
- Mineral mining
- Nuts
- Oil
- Peanuts
- Poultry
- Salt
- Shellfish
- Vegetables

TENNESSEE

Tennessee

Huntsville

Birmingham

Coosa

MISSISSIPPI

GEORGIA

Tombigbee

Alabama

★ Montgomery

Chattahoochee

N
W    E
S

0    40 Miles
0    40 Kilometers

Mobile

FLORIDA

GULF OF MEXICO

- Urban area
- Farming
- Forests, some farming
- Grazing, rangeland
- Swampland, some farming

## SEE IT HERE!

**ALABAMA MINING MUSEUM**

You can learn all about the history of Alabama's mining industry at the Alabama Mining Museum in the town of Dora. This is the state's official coal mining museum. It focuses on mining practices between 1890 and 1940, and features a 1900s train, as well as mining cars.

timberland. Houses, schools, and office buildings are built from Alabama pines, oaks, hickories, and ash. The lumber becomes desks, beds, and kitchen tables. The timber industry in Alabama is big. In fact, the state's timber industry ranks second in the United States, just behind Oregon's, and has billions of trees. While the timber industry cuts and mills millions of trees yearly, those same companies also plant and nurture new trees to renew the forests.

Coal mining put Alabama on the industrial map. The Cahaba Coal Field filled railroad cars running between West Blocton and Birmingham. Alabama's coal heated homes and fueled the state's major steel industry. The big boom in coal mining came between 1900 and 1929. Mining towns popped up along rail lines, and mining companies provided employees with houses, schools, churches, and stores. Coal mining still contributes to Alabama's economy. Since the first coal was mined more than a century ago, Alabama's mines have yielded 564 million tons of coal.

Alabama also has active limestone, marble, sand, and gravel quarries. These materials make everything from statues and tombstones to concrete, driveways, and building stone. The state has 45 oil or gas mines, as well as industries that support those businesses—factories that

# Top Products

**Agriculture** Poultry, cattle, nursery and sod products, cotton, peanuts, soybeans, hay, corn, wheat, potatoes, pecans, sweet potatoes

**Manufacturing** Paper products, chemicals, textiles, mining, food products, clothing, wood products, printing, motor vehicles, transportation equipment

**Mining** Oil, coal, iron ore, sulfur, salt, tin, copper, gold, limestone, gravel, clay

**Services** Hotels and lodging, personal and business services, health care, education, legal services

make mining equipment, transportation equipment, and pumps.

## MANUFACTURING AND DISTRIBUTION

Since soon after the end of the Civil War, Alabama has been a bustling industrial center. Today, more than 5,200 manufacturing and distribution facilities employ more than 312,000 workers. Twenty-four of those factories are manufacturing headquarters, and another 49 national and international corporations have business headquarters in Alabama. Across the state, 28,666 African Americans own their own businesses. The state ranks 14th in the nation in black-owned enterprises.

Industry in Alabama is a worldwide venture. Some 200 international companies, representing 23 countries, have plants in the state. Alabamians sell to a worldwide marketplace as well—shipping auto parts and oilseeds (seeds used to make cooking oil), aircraft and spacecraft, and lumber and plastics around the world.

Medical programs at the University of Alabama make Birmingham an important research city. Auburn University in Auburn has recently created a center for the study of alternative fuels. Alabama has produced world-class scientists, such as inventor George Washington Carver and Edward O. Wilson, a world-renowned entomologist (someone who studies insects).

**MINI-BIO**

## DANIEL PRATT, ALABAMA'S FIRST INDUSTRIALIST

He first worked as a carpenter, but Daniel Pratt (1799–1873) made his mark as an industrialist. Born in New Hampshire, Pratt settled in Alabama in 1833, convinced that Alabama could be home to manufacturing as well as agriculture. There he put his own money on the line. He and a partner began producing cotton gins and supplying parts for the gins. He also invested in a sawmill, a grist mill, an iron foundry, and a textile mill, and built blast furnaces that started Alabama as a producer of **pig iron**. Just after the Civil War, Pratt helped establish a thriving iron and steel industry in the state.

**?** **Want to know more?** See www.archives.state. al.us/famous/d_pratt.html

### WORD TO KNOW

**pig iron** *iron that is produced by a furnace using pressurized air and used to make steel and wrought iron, a relatively pure form of iron that can be forged and welded*

## MINI-BIO

### MAE JEMISON: WOMAN IN SPACE

She's a chemical engineer, a medical doctor, a scientist, a researcher, and an astronaut!

Mae Jemison (1956–) was born in Decatur, Alabama, and moved to Chicago as a young girl. An excellent student, she received a scholarship to attend Stanford University at age 16. After earning degrees from Stanford University and Cornell Medical College, Jemison entered the NASA space program in 1987. She has worked at the Kennedy Space Center in Florida and was on the space shuttle mission STS-47 Spacelab J in September 1992. This was a joint mission between the United States and Japan to research the effects of space flight on different life-forms. Jemison was the first African American woman in space. She now runs her own company, which develops advanced technologies.

**? Want to know more?** See http://quest.nasa.gov/space/frontiers/jemison.html

Aerospace in Huntsville, Alabama, is a multitiered industry. Research and development covers everything from space missions to the Hubble telescope. Space Camp brings in dozens of teens each year, and the Huntsville facility draws tourists from around the world. Wherever there is a major industry, support services flourish, and Huntsville is no different. Restaurants, hotels, dry cleaners, computer tech companies, and other support services thrive because the

Space Camp is located at the U.S. Space and Rocket Center in Huntsville.

Diners enjoy a Mexican meal at a Huntsville restaurant.

aerospace industry employs so many people. Jan Davis and Mae Jemison are two Alabamians who have traveled into space.

## DOING BUSINESS IN ALABAMA

Alabama features a number of economic advantages for incoming businesses. Many manufacturers who develop plants in Alabama enjoy **tax breaks**, convenient transportation, and well-trained employees. The state's many technical schools work with businesses to train future employees in needed skills.

Alabama's well-developed system of transportation is a big advantage for businesses. There are 23,500 miles (37,800 km) of federal highways, including five interstate highways, that connect the state's major cities with neighboring states. Five major railroad lines service the state, and Birmingham's international airport has connections to all major North American cities and several international sites. The port of Mobile currently serves as a global deepwater port, serving oceangoing

### WORD TO KNOW

**tax breaks** *credits or deductions in the amount of taxes owed; often given to encourage certain types of development or business*

boats of 130 major steamer lines. Containers filled with upstate lumber travel over the interstate to Mobile, are lifted onto freight ships, and head off to ports in Europe, South America, and Asia.

# What Do Alabamians Do?

This color-coded chart shows what industries Alabamians work in.

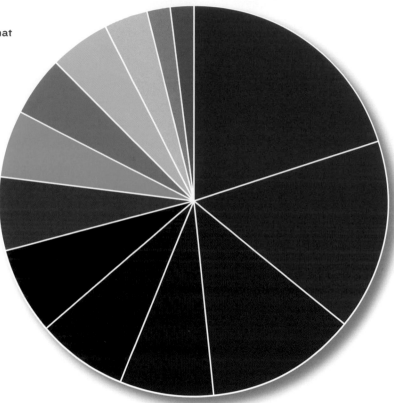

| | |
|---|---|
| **20.1%** | Educational services, and health care, and social assistance, 399,603 |
| **15.8%** | Manufacturing, 313,319 |
| **12.7%** | Retail trade, 251,626 |
| **7.6%** | Construction, 151,318 |
| **7.5%** | Professional, scientific, and management, and administrative and waste management services, 149,205 |
| **7.3%** | Arts, entertainment, and recreation, and accommodation, and food services, 145,008 |
| **6.1%** | Finance and insurance, and real estate and rental and leasing, 121,709 |
| **5.4%** | Transportation and warehousing, and utilities, 106,688 |
| **5.1%** | Public administration, 100,535 |
| **4.9%** | Other services, except public administration, 96,712 |
| **3.8%** | Wholesale trade, 75,863 |
| **1.9%** | Agriculture, forestry, fishing and hunting, and mining, 37,403 |
| **1.8%** | Information, 35,278 |

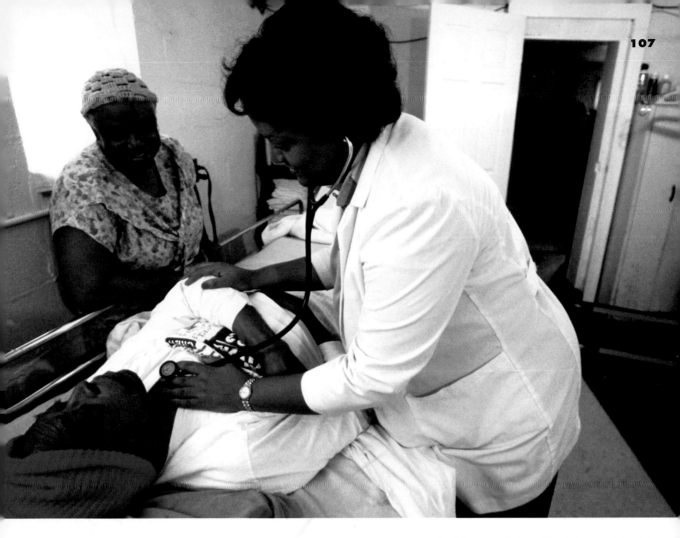

A doctor treats a patient at a rural health clinic in Bayou La Batre.

Two hundred years ago, nearly all Alabamians farmed the land. Others ran small shops, arranged transportation—by horse or oxen—or hunted for a living. Today, about one-fifth of Alabamians provide services such as computer programming, nursing, teaching, or cleaning. Another one-fifth work in retail trade, selling everything from T-shirts to tables to candy bars. The people who work in manufacturing make up 18 percent of the state's workers.

In 2006, Alabama experienced its lowest unemployment rate in 30 years. As the state's workforce adapts to new industries, Alabama will continue to grow and thrive in the years to come.

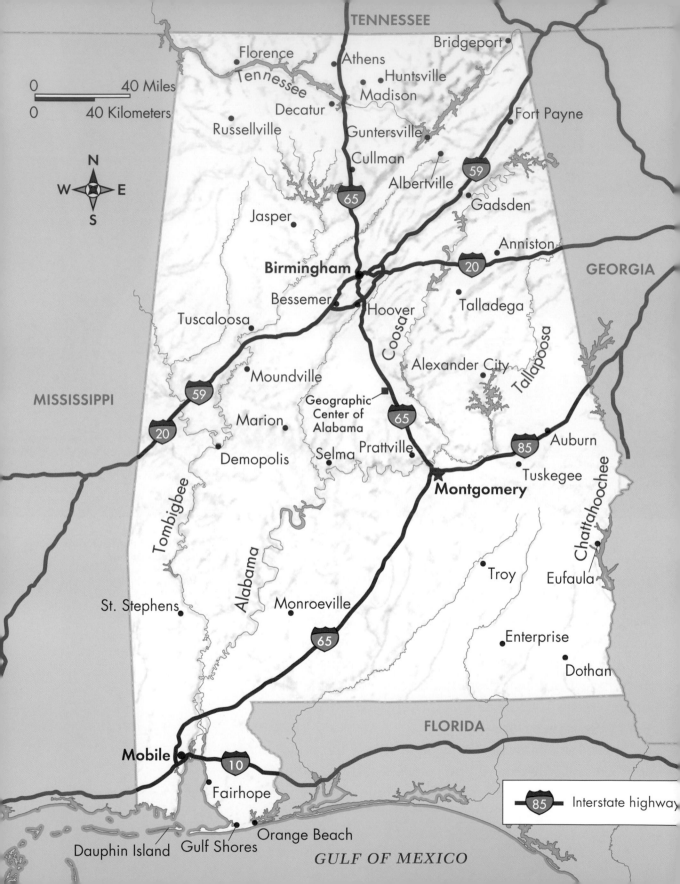

TENNESSEE

Bridgeport

Florence

Athens

Huntsville

Madison

Decatur

Fort Payne

Russellville

Guntersville

Cullman

59

Albertville

0        40 Miles

0        40 Kilometers

N
W        E
S

Jasper

Gadsden

Anniston

**Birmingham**

20

GEORGIA

Bessemer

Hoover

Talladega

Tuscaloosa

Coosa

MISSISSIPPI

Tallapoosa

59

Moundville

Alexander City

20

Marion

Geographic
Center of
Alabama

65

Demopolis

Selma

Prattville

85

Auburn

Tuskegee

**Montgomery**

Tombigbee

Chattahoochee

Alabama

St. Stephens

Monroeville

Troy

Eufaula

65

Enterprise

Dothan

FLORIDA

**Mobile**

10

Fairhope

Dauphin Island    Gulf Shores    Orange Beach

GULF OF MEXICO

85    Interstate highway

# CHAPTER NINE

**TRAVEL GUIDE**

# TRAVEL GUIDE

★

ALABAMA OFFERS OUTDOOR WONDERS, HISTORICAL SITES, AND CULTURAL SPOTS. Fans of the great outdoors should get out the bikes, canoes, kayaks, or hiking boots. Several areas offer spots to learn about the state's role in the Civil War and the civil rights movement. From folk arts to elegant museums, delights for the eyes abound. As for sports, choose from the roar of the crowds at hometown football or basketball games or the roar of engines at NASCAR races.

← Follow along with this travel map. We'll begin in Athens and travel all the way down to Mobile!

## MOUNTAIN REGION

**THINGS TO DO:** Take a walk back through history or have fun on a safari.

### Athens

★ **Alabama Veterans Museum and Archives:** This museum was established to preserve the memories of veterans from the Civil War to the present. Here you'll find memorabilia such as uniforms, medals, weapons, photos, books, tapes, and news clippings.

★ **Athens Town Square:** Tour historic Athens Town Square. Over the years, it has been burned and looted, and held center stage during the Civil War.

Burritt on the Mountain—A Living Museum

★ **Houston Memorial Library and Museum:** This 1835 house is the former home of attorney, U.S. senator, and two-time governor of Alabama George S. Houston. It features Houston family furnishings and a history room.

### Guntersville

★ **Guntersville Museum and Cultural Center:** This museum's permanent collection includes Indian artifacts, an exhibit on constructing Guntersville Dam, an extensive gem collection, a Guntersville Lake exhibit, and examples of local art and artifacts.

★ **Guntersville Railroad Depot and Museum:** With a miniature train display, this museum offers phenomenal railroad memorabilia from years past.

### Huntsville

★ **Burritt on the Mountain—A Living Museum:** From Burritt Mansion to a historic park and nature trails, this museum interprets Tennessee Valley life from the 1850s to the present.

EarlyWorks Children's Museum

★ **EarlyWorks Children's Museum:**
Visitors interact with history at this hands-on museum, which features a 46-foot (15 m) keelboat, a log cabin, and a general store.

★ **Huntsville Museum of Art:**
Located in downtown Huntsville within Big Spring International Park, the musem holds an extensive collection of American art.

★ **Alabama Constitution Village:**
This living-history museum re-creates a working village from the period 1805 to 1819. Tour the cabinetmaker's shop, print shop, confectionary shop, library, and post office. The village commemorates the place where the 1819 constitutional convention was held.

★ **Harmony Park Safari:** Get out your binoculars and your field guide. Here you'll see bison, camels, ostriches, pythons, rams, zebras, alligators, and more.

## METROPOLITAN REGION

**THINGS TO DO: Indulge your need for speed (race cars, that is), big-city living, and great music.**

### Birmingham

★ **Alabama Jazz Hall of Fame:**
This museum honors jazz greats with ties to Alabama, including Lionel Hampton, Erskine Hawkins, and Sun Ra. Visitors are taken from the beginning of jazz to the present day.

★ **Alabama Sports Hall of Fame and Museum:** Interactive exhibits and original memorabilia from over 200 inductees, including Coach Paul "Bear" Bryant, boxer Joe Louis, and track-and-field greats Jesse Owens and Carl Lewis.

★ **Birmingham Civil Rights Institute:** State-of-the-art multimedia exhibitions describe and interpret the days of post–World War I racial segregation to present-day racial progress.

★ **Birmingham Zoo:** More than 800 wild animals live at this zoo. You can see an alligator swamp, feed colorful parrots in Lorikeet Aviary, or experience an African savanna.

★ **Alabama Theatre for the Performing Arts:** This 1927 movie palace has been maintained in its original form. Built by Paramount, it now functions as a performing arts facility and houses the largest Wurlitzer pipe organ in the South.

## Talladega

★ **International Motorsports Hall of Fame:** At the hall of fame you'll see classic stock cars and memorabilia dating to 1902. Tour the Talladega Superspeedway right next door, where the library and archives preserve the history of auto racing!

★ **Talladega National Forest:** More than 7,500 acres (3,000 ha) of forest and wilderness are open to the public for camping and hiking.

## Tuscaloosa

★ **Alabama Museum of Natural History:** The collection includes displays of fossils, rocks, and minerals from the age of dinosaurs, ice age, and coal age, plus the only meteorite known to have struck a human!

★ **University of Alabama:** Tour this beautiful campus, and learn about the history of the university, which was founded in 1831. Among its historic landmarks are the Paul W. Bryant Museum of UA football and the Gorgas House.

★ **The Westervelt Warner Museum of American Art:** Hundreds of historic paintings, sculptures, and artifacts are on exhibit.

# RIVER HERITAGE REGION

**THINGS TO DO:** Visit civil rights landmarks, tour the Alabama state capitol, or see a college football game.

## Montgomery

★ **Alabama State Capitol:** Tour Alabama's historic state capitol. Be sure to notice the star on the capitol steps outside, which marks the spot where Jefferson Davis was sworn in as president of the Confederate States of America.

Civil Rights Memorial Center

★ **Civil Rights Memorial Center:**
Here you can honor the memories
of those who gave their lives in the
struggle for civil rights and pledge
your name to the Wall of Tolerance.

★ **Hank Williams Museum:** Visit
this shrine to the country music
legend Hank Williams. It features
his 1952 Cadillac in which he made
his final journey, along with clothing he performed in and other
memorabilia.

★ **First White House of the
Confederacy:** Tour the historic house that was home to
Confederate president Jefferson
Davis and family while the capitol
was in Montgomery. Built in 1835,
the home also displays furnishings
from the 1850s and 1860s.

★ **Montgomery Museum of Fine
Arts:** This excellent fine arts
museum houses a permanent collection of 19th- and 20th-century
American paintings and sculpture,
southern regional art, Old Master
prints, and decorative arts.

★ **Rosa Parks Library and
Museum:** Through interactive multimedia exhibits, this state-of-the-art
museum spotlights events that led
to the Montgomery bus boycott and
the early civil rights movement.

Rosa Parks Museum and Children's Wing

★ **The MOOseum:** This Montgomery
museum is devoted to the history of
beef and cattle.

## Auburn

★ **Auburn University:** Stroll the lovely 1,871-acre (757 ha) campus. And be sure to visit the Jonathan Bell Lovelace Athletic Museum and Hall of Honor to learn more about the spirit of Auburn University.

## SEE IT HERE!

### BOLL WEEVIL MONUMENT

An odd, vaguely Grecian statue topped by an extra-large likeness of a boll weevil stands 13 feet (4 m) tall in Enterprise. When cotton was the only real revenue maker in the area, the boll weevil began eating its way through all of the cotton crops. This infestation ruined a whole year's cotton crop and caused an economic depression in the area. Farmers realized that they were going to need to diversify their crops if they were going to survive and started planting peanuts.

The Boll Weevil Monument stands as the only monument to an agricultural pest, and as a tribute to how something devastating can be the cause for great change.

Boll weevil monument

## Selma

★ **National Voting Rights Museum and Institute:** This museum offers a pictorial history of the voting rights struggle. On display is a record of the events and people who made civil rights history.

★ **Old Depot Museum:** Housed in an 1891 railway depot, this history museum displays artifacts from pre-historic Alabama to the voting rights era. It also features a Civil War room, and a black heritage wing.

★ **Slavery and Civil War Museum:** This sister museum to the National Voting Rights Museum features exhibits that explore the impact of slavery on American history.

## GULF COAST REGION

**THINGS TO DO:** Visit historic museums or spend a day on white, sandy beaches.

## Monroeville

★ **Alabama River Heritage Museum:** Travel back to 60 million years ago, and see fossils from the Claiborne Bluff. The museum also features Native American artifacts and steamboat replicas.

★ **Old Courthouse Museum:** This historic courthouse was used as a model for the trial scene in the film *To Kill A Mockingbird*. If you visit in the spring, you may catch a performance of the unforgettable trial scene.

## Dauphin Island

★ **Audubon Bird Sanctuary:** Tour this 160-acre (65 ha) sanctuary along a trail system that leads you past a beautiful freshwater lake, dunes, gulf beaches, a swamp, and a hardwood forest. Dauphin Island is one of the top birding locations in the nation.

★ **Fort Gaines and Fort Morgan:** This is the location of an 1864 Civil War battle.

## Orange Beach

★ **Orange Beach Indian and Sea Museum:** This museum is dedicated to the ongoing preservation of the Gulf Coast and the Native American history of the area. The museum features an old schoolhouse and original furnishings.

## Mobile

★ **Bragg-Mitchell Mansion:** This 20-room mansion, built in 1855, is one of the Gulf Coast's grandest estates.

★ **Mobile Carnival Museum:** Mobile hosts the oldest Mardi Gras celebration in the United States. At this museum, you can view a wealth of memorabilia, including crowns, scepters, floats, and jeweled robes.

★ **Mobile Zoo:** This nonprofit wildlife park was established to educate visitors about wildlife from all over the world. You'll see zebras, wolves, baboons, and lynx just to name a few. You can also enjoy a hayride and a petting zoo.

★ **Bellingrath Gardens:** Explore the grounds year round at this 65-acre (26 ha) estate. These dramatic gardens include the Bayou Boardwalk, a butterfly garden, and the Asian-American Gardens.

Bellingrath Gardens

## WRITING PROJECTS

Check out these ideas for creating election brochures and writing you-are-there editorials.

**118**

## ART PROJECTS

**119**

You can learn about the st quarter and design your o illustrate the state song, or create a dazzling PowerP presentation.

## TIMELINE

What happened when? This timeline highlights important events in the state's history—and shows what was happening throughout the United States at the same time.

**122**

## FAST FACTS

Use this section to find fascinating facts about state symbols, land area and population statistics, weather, sports teams, and much more.

**126**

## GLOSSARY

Remember the Words to Know from the chapters in this book? They're all collected here.

**125**

# SCIENCE, TECHNOLOGY, & MATH PROJECTS

ake weather maps, graph population statistics, and earch endangered species that live in the state.

## 120

# PRIMARY VS. SECONDARY SOURCES

## 121

So what are primary and secondary sources, and what's the diff? This section explains all that and where you can find them.

# BIOGRAPHICAL DICTIONARY

## 133

This at-a-glance guide highlights some of the state's most important and influential people. Visit this section and read about their contributions to the state, the country, and the world.

# RESOURCES

Books, Web sites, DVDs, and more. Take a look at these additional sources for information about the state.

## 137

# WRITING PROJECTS

★ ★ ★

## Write a Memoir, Journal, or Editorial for Your School Newspaper!
**Picture Yourself . . .**

. . . as a member of the Creek or Choctaw nation during the Creek War. Think about what divided the groups during this bitter conflict. Create a journal recording your experiences, or write an editorial for your school paper.

**SEE:** Chapter Four, pages 48–49.

**GO TO:** Visit the Web site for Horseshoe Bend National Military Park in Daviston, Alabama, at www.nps.gov/archive/hobe/home/creekwar.htm for more information about the Creek War.

. . . as a participant in the civil rights movement. From the brave actions taken by individuals such as Rosa Parks and Martin Luther King Jr. to the collective strength of ordinary citizens who joined together, the struggle for civil rights in Alabama and the United States teaches us important lessons about how individuals can effect social change. Imagine yourself on a civil rights march in Alabama. Keep a journal of your experiences, such as the speeches you heard and the resistance you encountered. What kept you going?

**SEE:** Chapter Five, pages 66–70.

**GO TO:** Visit the National Association for the Advancement of Colored People Web site at www. naacp.org to find out more about the history of the organization and its role in the civil rights movement.

## Create an Election Brochure or Web Site!
**Run for office!**

Throughout this book you've read about some of the issues that concern Alabama today. As a candidate for governor of Alabama, create a campaign brochure or Web site. Explain how you meet the qualifications to be governor of Alabama and talk about the three or four major issues you'll focus on if you're elected. Remember, you'll be responsible for Alabama's budget. How would you spend the taxpayers' money?

**SEE:** Chapter Seven, page 88.

**GO TO:** Want to know more about what it takes to run the state? Go to Alabama's Government Web site at www.alabama.gov.

## Compare and Contrast —When, Why, and How Did they Come?

Compare the migration and explorations of Alabama's first Native people and its first Europeans. Tell about:
★ when their migrations began
★ how they traveled
★ why they migrated
★ where their journeys began and ended
★ what they found when they arrived

**SEE:** Chapters Two and Three, pages 26–43.

# ART PROJECTS

★ ▲ ▲

## Create a PowerPoint Presentation or Visitors' Guide

**Welcome to Alabama!**

Alabama's a great place to visit, and to live! From its natural beauty to its bustling cities and historic sites, there's plenty to see and do. In your PowerPoint presentation or brochure, highlight 10 to 15 of Alabama landmarks. Be sure to include: a map of the state showing where these sites are located, photos, illustrations, Web links, natural history facts, geographic stats, climate and weather info, and descriptions of plants and wildlife.

**SEE:** Chapter One, pages 6–24 and Chapter Nine, pages 108–115.

**GO TO:** Visit the official Web site of Alabama tourism at www.tourAlabama.org. Download and print maps, photos, national landmark images, and vacation ideas for tourists.

## Illustrate the Lyrics to the Alabama State Song

**("Alabama")**

Use markers, paints, photos, collage, colored pencils, or computer graphics to illustrate the lyrics to "Alabama," the state song. Turn your illustrations into a picture book, or scan them into a PowerPoint presentation and add music.

**SEE:** The lyrics to "Alabama" on page 128.

**GO TO:** Visit the Alabama state Web site at www.alabama.gov to find out more about the origin of the Alabama state song, "Alabama."

## Research Alabama's State Quarter

From 1999 to 2008, the U.S. Mint introduced new quarters commemorating each of the 50 states in the order that they were admitted into the Union. Each state's quarter features a unique design on its reverse, or back.

**GO TO:** www.usmint.gov/kids and find out what's featured on the back of the Alabama quarter.

Research and write an essay explaining:

★ the significance of each image

★ who designed the quarter

★ who chose the final design

Design your own Alabama state quarter. What images would you choose for the reverse?

★ Make a poster showing the Alabama quarter and label each image.

# SCIENCE, TECHNOLOGY, & MATH PROJECTS

★ ★ ★

## Graph Population Statistics!

★ Compare population statistics (such as ethnic background, birth, death, and literacy rates) in Alabama counties or major cities.

★ In your graph or chart, look at population density, and write sentences describing what the population statistics show; graph one set of population statistics, and write a paragraph explaining what the graphs reveal.

**SEE:** Chapter Six, pages 72–76.

**GO TO:** Check out the official Web site for the U.S. Census Bureau at www.census.gov, and at http://quickfacts.census.gov/qfd/states/01000.html, to find out more about population statistics, how they work, and the statistics for Alabama.

## Create a Weather Map of Alabama!

Use your knowledge of Alabama's geography to research and identify conditions that result in specific weather events, including thunderstorms, tropical storms, and hurricanes. What is it about the geography of Alabama that makes it vulnerable to things like hurricanes? Create a weather map or poster that shows the weather patterns over the state. Include a caption explaining the technology used to measure various weather phenomena such as hurricanes, and provide data.

**SEE:** Chapter One, pages 18–21.

**GO TO:** The National Oceanic and Atmospheric Administration's National Weather Service Web site at www.weather.gov for weather maps and forecasts for Alabama.

## Track Endangered Species

Using your knowledge of Alabama's wildlife, research what animals and plants are endangered or threatened. Find out what the state is doing to protect these species. Chart known populations of the animals and plants, and report on changes in certain geographic areas.

**SEE:** Chapter One, page 24–25.

**GO TO:** Sites such as www.outdooralabama.com/education/students/T&E.cfm

Enjoying a Mexican meal

# PRIMARY VS SECONDARY SOURCES

★  ★  ★

## What's the Diff?

**Your teacher may require at least one or two primary sources and one or two secondary sources for your assignment.** So, what's the difference between the two?

★ **Primary sources are original.** You are reading the actual words of someone's diary, journal, letter, autobiography or interview. Primary sources can also be photographs, maps, prints, cartoons, news/film footage, posters, first-person newspaper articles, drawings, musical scores, and recordings. By the way, when you conduct a survey, interview someone, shoot a video or take photographs to include in a project, you are creating primary sources!

★ **Secondary sources are what you find in encyclopedias, textbooks, articles, biographies, and almanacs.** These are written by a person or group of people who tell about something that happened to someone else. Secondary sources also recount what another person said or did. This book is an example of a secondary source.

## Now that you know what primary sources are—where can you find them?

★ **Your school or local library:** Check the library catalog for collections of original writings, government documents, musical scores, and so on. Some of this material may be stored on microfilm. The Library of Congress Web site (www.loc.gov) is an excellent online resource for primary source materials.

★ **Historical societies:** These organizations keep historical documents, photographs, and other materials. Staff members can help you find what you are looking for. History museums are also great places to see primary sources firsthand.

★ **The Internet:** There are lots of sites that have primary sources you can download and use in a project or assignment.

# TIMELINE

★ ★ ★

**U.S. Events** | 300 | **Alabama Events**

**300–1540**
Native American tribes thrive in Alabama.

1400

1500

**1492**
Christopher Columbus and his crew sight land in the Caribbean Sea.

**1519**
Alonzo de Piñeda sails into the Gulf of Mexico.

**1540**
Hernando de Soto leads an expedition into today's Alabama.

**1565**
Spanish admiral Pedro Menéndez de Avilés founds St. Augustine, Florida, the oldest continuously occupied European settlement in the continental United States.

1600

**1699**
The Le Moyne brothers enter Mobile Bay.

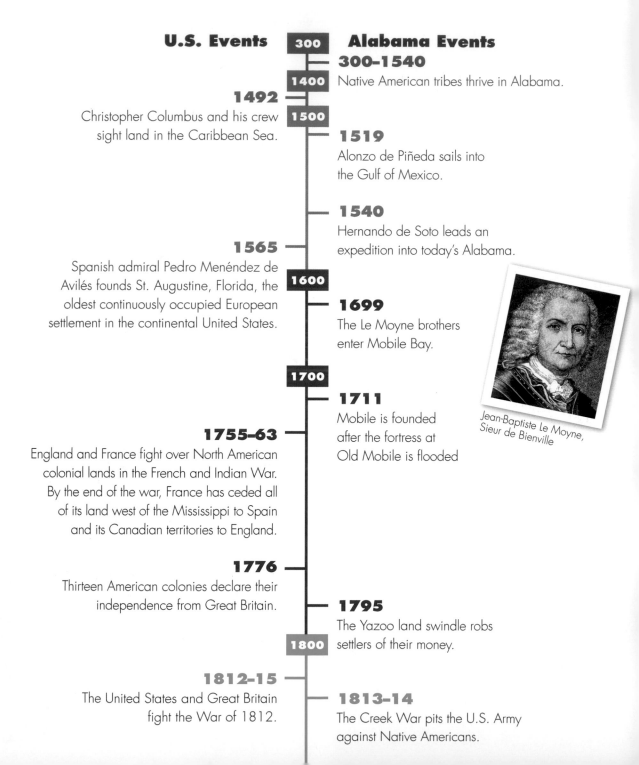

Jean-Baptiste Le Moyne, Sieur de Bienville

1700

**1711**
Mobile is founded after the fortress at Old Mobile is flooded

**1755–63**
England and France fight over North American colonial lands in the French and Indian War. By the end of the war, France has ceded all of its land west of the Mississippi to Spain and its Canadian territories to England.

**1776**
Thirteen American colonies declare their independence from Great Britain.

**1795**
The Yazoo land swindle robs settlers of their money.

1800

**1812–15**
The United States and Great Britain fight the War of 1812.

**1813–14**
The Creek War pits the U.S. Army against Native Americans.

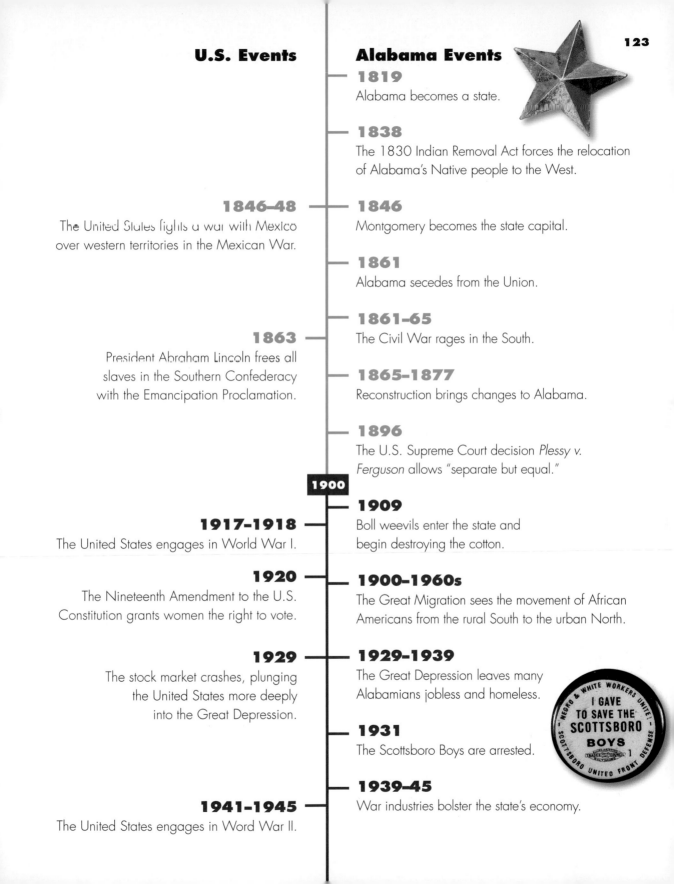

**U.S. Events**

**Alabama Events**

**1819**
Alabama becomes a state.

**1838**
The 1830 Indian Removal Act forces the relocation of Alabama's Native people to the West.

**1846–48**
The United States fights a war with Mexico over western territories in the Mexican War.

**1846**
Montgomery becomes the state capital.

**1861**
Alabama secedes from the Union.

**1861–65**
The Civil War rages in the South.

**1863**
President Abraham Lincoln frees all slaves in the Southern Confederacy with the Emancipation Proclamation.

**1865–1877**
Reconstruction brings changes to Alabama.

**1896**
The U.S. Supreme Court decision *Plessy v. Ferguson* allows "separate but equal."

**1900**

**1909**
Boll weevils enter the state and begin destroying the cotton.

**1917–1918**
The United States engages in World War I.

**1920**
The Nineteenth Amendment to the U.S. Constitution grants women the right to vote.

**1900–1960s**
The Great Migration sees the movement of African Americans from the rural South to the urban North.

**1929**
The stock market crashes, plunging the United States more deeply into the Great Depression.

**1929–1939**
The Great Depression leaves many Alabamians jobless and homeless.

**1931**
The Scottsboro Boys are arrested.

**1939–45**
War industries bolster the state's economy.

**1941–1945**
The United States engages in Word War II.

## U.S. Events

## Alabama Events

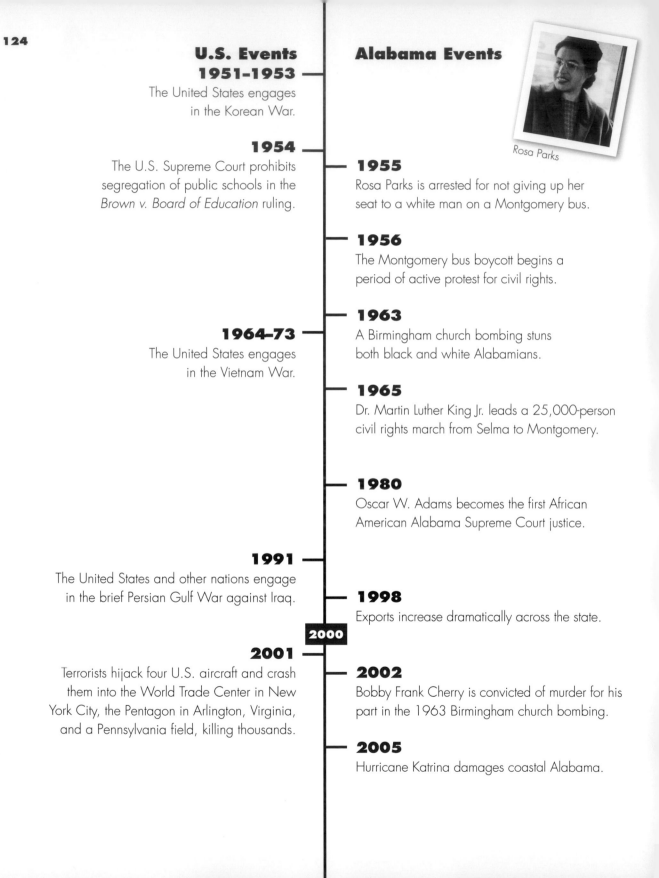

*Rosa Parks*

**1951–1953**
The United States engages in the Korean War.

**1954**
The U.S. Supreme Court prohibits segregation of public schools in the *Brown v. Board of Education* ruling.

**1955**
Rosa Parks is arrested for not giving up her seat to a white man on a Montgomery bus.

**1956**
The Montgomery bus boycott begins a period of active protest for civil rights.

**1963**
A Birmingham church bombing stuns both black and white Alabamians.

**1964–73**
The United States engages in the Vietnam War.

**1965**
Dr. Martin Luther King Jr. leads a 25,000-person civil rights march from Selma to Montgomery.

**1980**
Oscar W. Adams becomes the first African American Alabama Supreme Court justice.

**1991**
The United States and other nations engage in the brief Persian Gulf War against Iraq.

**1998**
Exports increase dramatically across the state.

**2000**

**2001**
Terrorists hijack four U.S. aircraft and crash them into the World Trade Center in New York City, the Pentagon in Arlington, Virginia, and a Pennsylvania field, killing thousands.

**2002**
Bobby Frank Cherry is convicted of murder for his part in the 1963 Birmingham church bombing.

**2005**
Hurricane Katrina damages coastal Alabama.

# GLOSSARY

★ ★ ★

**anthropologists** people who study the development of human cultures

**archaeologists** people who study the remains of past human societies

**bonds** interest-bearing loan agreements made to raise specific amounts of money in a specified period of time

**confederacy** a group that is formed for shared support and common goals

**constitution** a written document that contains all the governing principles of a state or country

**correctional** of or dealing with criminals, particularly prisons, parole, and rehabilitation

**glaciers** slow-moving masses of ice

**guerrilla** a type of warfare that is fought by soldiers who are not sponsored by a recognized government

**lynching** to kill by mob without a lawful trial

**pig iron** iron that is produced by a furnace using pressurized air and used to make steel and wrought iron, a relatively pure form of iron that can be forged and welded

**precipitation** all water that falls to the earth, including rain, sleet, hail, snow, dew, fog, or mist

**prophet** a person who knows God's will or can predict the future

**sediment** material eroded from rocks and deposited elsewhere by wind, water, or glaciers

**segregated** separated from others, according to race, class, ethnic group, religion, or other factors

**shape-note singing** a tradition of church singing using hymns written with shaped notes, so singers don't have to be able to read music to participate; usually done without instrument accompaniment

**sharecropping** farming another person's land in exchange for a portion of the profits minus the landowner's cost for providing equipment and living quarters

**shoals** sandbanks or sandbars that make water shallow

**sit-ins** acts of protest that involve sitting in racially segregated places and refusing to leave

**stalactite** a column or pillar formed on the roof of a cave from dripping groundwater

**stalagmite** a column or pillar formed on the floor of a cave from dripping groundwater

**tax breaks** credits or deductions in the amount of taxes owed; often given to encourage certain types of development or business

# FAST FACTS

★  ★  ★

## State Symbols

| | |
|---|---|
| **Statehood date** | December 14, 1819, the 22nd state |
| **Origin of state name** | From the Native American tribe of the same name, which is believed to be a combination of two Chickasaw words meaning vegetation (*alba*) and gatherer (*amo*) |
| **State capital** | Montgomery |
| **State nickname** | No official nickname (though commonly referred to as the "Heart of Dixie" and the "Cotton State") |
| **State motto** | *Audemus Jura Nostra Defendere* ("We Dare Defend Our Rights") |
| **State bird** | Yellowhammer |
| **State flower** | Camellia |
| **State saltwater fish** | Tarpon |
| **State freshwater fish** | Large-mouth bass |
| **State mineral** | Hematite (red iron ore) |
| **State rock** | Marble |
| **State gemstone** | Star blue quartz |
| **State song** | "Alabama" See page 128 |
| **State tree** | Southern longleaf pine |
| **State fossil** | *Basilosaurus cetoides* |
| **State insect** | Monarch butterfly |
| **State horse** | Racking horse |
| **State game bird** | Wild turkey |
| **State American folk dance** | Square dance |
| **State nut** | Pecan |
| **State shell** | *Scaphella junonia johnstoneae* |
| **State fair** | Montgomery (early October) |

State seal

State flag

# Geography

| | |
|---|---|
| **Total area; rank** | 52,419 square miles (135,765 sq km); 30th |
| **Land; rank** | 50,744 square miles (131,426 sq km); 28th |
| **Water; rank** | 1,675 square miles (4,338 sq km); 23rd |
| **Inland water; rank** | 956 square miles (2,476 sq km); 23rd |
| **Coastal water; rank** | 519 square miles (1,344 sq km); 12th |
| **Territorial water; rank** | 200 square miles (518 sq km); 18th |
| **Geographic center** | Chilton, 12 miles (19 km) southwest of Clanton |
| **Latitude** | 84° 51' N to 88° 28' N |
| **Longitude** | 30° 13' W to 35° W |
| **Highest point** | Cheaha Mountain, 2,405 feet (733 m) |
| **Lowest point** | Sea level along the Gulf of Mexico |
| **Largest city** | Birmingham |
| **Number of counties** | 67 |
| **Longest river** | Alabama |

# Population

| | |
|---|---|
| **Population; rank (2006 estimate)** | 4,599,030; 23rd |
| **Density (2006 estimate)** | 91 persons per square mile (35 per sq km) |
| **Population distribution (2000 census)** | 55% urban, 45% rural |
| **Ethnic distribution (2005 estimate)** | White persons: 71.4%* |
| | Black persons: 26.4%* |
| | Asian persons: 0.8%* |
| | American Indian and Alaska Native persons: 0.5%* |
| | Native Hawaiian and Other Pacific Islander: 0.0%* |
| | Persons reporting two or more races: 0.9% |
| | Persons of Hispanic or Latino origin: 2.3%† |
| | White persons not Hispanic: 69.3% |

*Includes persons reporting only one race.*
*† Hispanics may be of any race, so they are also included in applicable race categories.*

# Weather

| | |
|---|---|
| **Record high temperature** | 112°F (44°C) at Centreville on September 5, 1925 |
| **Record low temperature** | −27°F (−33°C) at New Market on January 30, 1966 |
| **Average July temperature** | 82°F (28°C) |
| **Average January temperature** | 51°F (10°C) |
| **Average annual precipitation** | 66 inches (168 cm) |

# STATE SONG

★ ★ ★

## *"Alabama"*
Words by Julia S. Tutwiler
Music by Edna Goeckel Gussen

The words of "Alabama" were written by Julia S. Tutwiler, a distinguished educator and humanitarian. The inspiration for writing "Alabama" came to Tutwiler in the late 1860s after a trip to Germany, where she had been studying new educational methods for girls and women. In Germany, she saw that patriotism was kept aflame by spirited songs. So she decided to write one for her native state. The State Federation of Music Clubs adopted the music, by Edna Gockel Gussen of Birmingham. On March 9, 1931, the Alabama state legislature officially adopted the music and words as the state song of Alabama.

Alabama, Alabama,
We will aye be true to thee,
From thy Southern shore where groweth,
By the sea thine orange tree.
To thy Northern vale where floweth,
Deep and blue thy Tennessee,
Alabama, Alabama,
We will aye be true to thee!

Broad thy stream whose name thou bearest;
Grand thy Bigbee rolls along,
Fair thy Coosa-Tallapoosa,
Bold thy Warrior, dark and strong,
Goodlier than the land that Moses
Climbed lone Nebo's Mount to see,
Alabama, Alabama,
We will aye be true to thee!

From thy prairies broad and fertile,
Where thy snow-white cotton shines.
To the hills where coal and iron
Hide in thy exhaustless mines,
Strong-armed miners—sturdy farmers:
Loyal hearts what'er we be.
Alabama, Alabama,
We will aye be true to thee!

From the quarries where the marble
White as that of Paros gleams
Waiting till thy sculptor's chisel,
Wake to life thy poet's dreams;
For not only wealth of nature,
Wealth of mind hast thou to fee,
Alabama, Alabama,
We will aye be true to thee!

Where the perfumed south-wind whispers,
Thy magnolia groves among,
Softer than a mother's kisses,
Sweeter than a mother's song;
Where the golden jasmine trailing,
Woos the treasure-laden bee,
Alabama, Alabama,
We will aye be true to thee!

Brave and pure thy men and women,
Better this than corn and wine
Make us worthy, God in Heaven
Of this goodly land of Thine;
Hearts as open as our doorways,
Liberal hands and spirits free,
Alabama, Alabama,
We will aye be true to thee!

Little, little can I give thee,
Alabama, mother mine;
But that little—hand, brain, spirit,
All I have and am are thine.
Take, O take, the gift and giver.
Take and serve thyself with me,
Alabama, Alabama,
I will aye be true to thee.

# NATURAL AREAS AND HISTORIC SITES

★ ★ ★

## National Monument

*Russell Cave National Monument* provided shelter to prehistoric peoples for more than 10,000 years and contains archaeological records of their cultures.

## National Historic Sites

*Tuskegee Institute National Historic Site* features the Tuskegee Normal and Industrial Institute, which was founded in 1881 to help further the education of African Americans.

*Tuskegee Airmen National Historic Site* is home to the first military training school for African American pilots.

## National Historic and Scenic Trails

*Selma to Montgomery National Historic Trail* follows the 54-mile (87 km) path taken by many to help secure equal rights.

*Trail of Tears National Historic Trail* is the route Native Americans were forced to take westward from their homelands.

## Other Sites Protected by the National Park Service

*Natchez Trace Parkway* and *Horseshoe Bend National Military Park* are a few of the many other sites preserved and protected by the National Park Service.

## National Forests

*Bankhead, Conecuh, Talladega,* and *Tuskegee* national forests include approximately 666,000 acres (270,000 ha) of land, covering varied terrain.

## State Parks and Forests

Alabama has 23 state parks. *Lake Guntersville State Park* and *Gulf State Park* are two of the largest.

# SPORTS TEAMS

★ ★ ★

## NCAA Teams (Division I)

Alabama A&M University *Bulldogs*
Alabama State University *Hornets*
Auburn University *Tigers*
Birmingham-Southern College *Panthers*
Jacksonville State University *Gamecocks*
Samford University *Bulldogs*
Troy State University *Trojans*
University of Alabama *Crimson Tide*
University of Alabama–Birmingham *Blazers*
University of South Alabama *Jaguars*

# CULTURAL INSTITUTIONS

## Libraries

*Amelia Gayle Gorgas Library* at the University of Alabama (Mobile) houses an outstanding collection of reference material on the history and culture of Alabama.

*Lister Hill Library* at the University of Alabama (Birmingham) is known for its historical medical collection.

## Museums

*Bellingrath Gardens* (Mobile) has stunning displays of spring azaleas and autumn chrysanthemums.

*The Birmingham Museum of Art* has a renowned collection of more than 21,000 works of art dating from ancient to modern times.

*The Montgomery Museum of Fine Arts* collects and preserves works of art by some of history's best-known artists and some of the region's best-loved artists.

*The Berman Museum* (Anniston) has a collection of 1,500 weapons that once belonged to people ranging from Napoleon I to Jefferson Davis.

*The Birmingham Civil Rights Museum* has exhibits depicting racial segregation of the 1920s through present-day civil rights progress.

*The U.S. Space and Rocket Center at Tranquility Base* (Huntsville) houses a large collection of spacecraft, rockets, and hands-on astronaut training exhibits.

## Performing Arts

Alabama has one major opera company, one major dance company, and one major professional theater company.

*Alabama Operaworks* is one of the fastest-growing opera companies in the Southeast.

*Alabama Dance Theatre* is a recognized and renowned dance company in the Southeast.

*The 13th Street Ensemble* is a professional theater company in residence at the Alys Stephens Center of the University of Alabama at Birmingham.

## Universities and Colleges

In 2006, Alabama had 40 public and 28 private institutions of higher learning.

# ANNUAL EVENTS

## January–March

**Mardi Gras** in Mobile (February–March)

**Azalea Spectacular** in Mobile (February–March)

**Selma Pilgrimage Weekend** (March)

## April–June

**Eufaula Pilgrimage** (April)

**Birmingham Festival of Arts** (April)

**Talladega 500** in Talladega (April)

**Zoo Weekend** in Montgomery (April)

**Birmingham Rose Show** (May)

**Panoply**, a festival of the visual and performing arts, in Huntsville (May)

**City Stages** in Birmingham (May)

**Jubilee Cityfest** in Montgomery (May)

**America's Junior Miss** in Mobile (late June)

**Chilton County Peach Festival** in Clanton (June)

## July–September

**W. C. Handy Music Festival** in Florence (late July–August)

**River Boat Regatta** in Guntersville (August)

**Big Spring Jam** in Huntsville (September)

## October–December

**South Alabama State Fair** in Montgomery (October)

**National Shrimp Festival** in Gulf Shores (October)

**EA Sports 500** in Talladega (October)

**National Peanut Festival** in Dothan (November)

**Annual Thanksgiving Day Pow Wow** in Atmore (November)

**Victorian Front Porch Christmas** in Opelika (December)

# BIOGRAPHICAL DICTIONARY

**Henry Louis "Hank" Aaron** See page 82.

**Ralph Abernathy (1926–1990)** was a clergyman and activist during the civil rights movement who worked with Martin Luther King Jr. He was born in Linden.

**Courteney Cox Arquette (1964–)** is best known for the role of Monica Geller in the television series *Friends*. She was born in Birmingham.

**Tallulah Brockman Bankhead (1903–1968)** was an actress who appeared in the film *Lifeboat* and on stage in *Little Foxes* and *The Skin of Our Teeth*. She was born in Huntsville.

**Jean-Baptiste Le Moyne, Sieur de Bienville** See page 42.

**Hugo LaFayette Black (1886–1971)** served as a U.S. Supreme Court justice from 1937 to 1971. He was born in Clay County.

**George Washington Carver** See page 100.

Nat King Cole

**Nat "King" Cole (1919–1965)** was a jazz and pop singer known for his renditions of "The Christmas Song" and "Unforgettable." He was born in Montgomery.

**Blanche Evans Dean** See page 24.

**Fannie Flagg (1944–)** is an actress and the author of *Fried Green Tomatoes at the Whistle Stop Café*. She was born in Birmingham.

**Vonetta Flowers (1973–)** is an American bobsledder. At the 2002 Winter Olympics, she won a gold medal in the two-woman bobsled event. She became the first black person to win a gold medal in the Winter Games. She was born in Birmingham.

**Winston Groom (1944–)** is a novelist best known for *Forrest Gump*. He grew up in Mobile.

**Mia Hamm-Garciaparra** See page 83.

Courteney Cox Arquette

**William Christopher "W. C." Handy** See page 77.

**Jeremiah Haralson (1846–c. 1916)**, was born into slavery, worked on an Alabama plantation, and taught himself to read and write. He was elected to the state legislature and in 1874 to Congress, where he supported voting rights for all men. He became the leading black politician in the state, a friend of Jefferson Davis, and spoke out for "peace between the two races."

**Emmylou Harris (1947–)** is a country music singer and songwriter. She was born in Birmingham.

**Erskine Hawkins (1914–1993)** was a trumpet player and big band leader from Birmingham. He is remembered for the jazz standard "Tuxedo Junction" (1939).

**Alexis Herman (1947–)** served as secretary of the U.S. Department of Labor from 1997 to 2001. She was born in Mobile.

**Taylor Hicks (1976–)** is a singer-songwriter who was born in Birmingham. Influenced by rock, blues, and soul, he is best known for winning the *American Idol* competition in 2006.

Coretta Scott King

**Lonnie Holley (1950–)** is an artist known for his sandstone carvings, paintings, and found-object sculptures. He was born in Birmingham.

**Vincent Edward "Bo" Jackson (1962–)** is an athlete who played both professional football and baseball. Born in Bessemer, he was the first person to be named an All-Star in both sports.

**Mae Jemison** See page 104.

**Percy Lavon Julian (1899–1975)** was an award-winning chemist and inventor who worked with soy proteins. He was born in Montgomery.

**Helen Adams Keller** See page 78.

**Coretta Scott King (1927–2006)** worked for civil rights and equality. Born in Marion, she was married to Martin Luther King Jr.

Emmylou Harris

**Martin Luther King Jr. (1929–1968)** was a civil rights leader. He was born in Atlanta, but served as pastor of the Dexter Avenue Baptist Church in Montgomery. He also helped lead the boycott of the Montgomery bus system. He won the Nobel Peace Prize in 1964.

**Harper Lee (1926–)** is the author of *To Kill a Mockingbird*, her only novel. She was born in Monroeville.

**Joe Louis (1914–1981)** was a boxer known as the Brown Bomber. He held the world championship in boxing for many years. He was born in Lexington.

**F. David Mathews (1935–)** is an educator who was born in Grove Hill. He was secretary of the U.S. Department of Heath, Education and Welfare from 1975 to 1977.

**Ida Brandon Mathis (1857–1925)**, born in Florence, was a farmer's daughter with a remarkable skill for producing profitable crops. Mathis was a champion of crop rotation. She developed a credit program that helped her fellow Alabama farmers succeed. Called the "economic Moses of the South," Mathis attracted industrial development to Alabama, providing jobs for many workers. In 1993, she became a member of the Alabama Women's Hall of Fame.

Jesse Owens

**Willie Howard Mays Jr. (1931–)**, known as the "Say Hey Kid," is a legendary Hall of Fame center fielder considered by many to be the greatest all-around baseball player of all time. Mays played for the New York and San Francisco Giants and the New York Mets. He was born in Westville.

**Clarence Bloomfield Moore** See page 30.

**Jesse Owens (1913–1980)** was an Olympic gold medalist in track and field. He stunned the Germans and Adolf Hitler at the 1936 Berlin Olympics by winning four events. He was born in Danville.

**Leroy Robert "Satchel" Paige (c. 1906–1982)** was a pitcher in the Negro Leagues and in Major League Baseball. He is considered one of the greatest pitchers of all time. Paige was born in Mobile.

**Rosa McCauley Parks** See page 67.

**Daniel Pratt** See page 103.

**Pushmataha** See page 48.

**James T. Rapier** See page 59.

**Condoleezza Rice** See page 92.

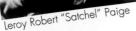
Leroy Robert "Satchel" Paige

**David Satcher (1941–)** served as the U.S. surgeon general from 1998 to 2002. He was born in Anniston.

**Benjamin Turner (1825–1894)**, who was born into slavery. served on the Selma city council and in 1870 was sent to Congress. He strongly supported loans to poor southern farmers, integrated schools, and civil rights.

**Tuscaloosa** See page 40.

**Julia Strudwick Tutwiler** See page 56.

**George Wallace Jr. (1919–1998)** was an Alabama governor and civil rights opponent who rose to national fame when he refused to desegregate Alabama schools despite federal orders to do so. He was born in Eufaula.

**Booker T. Washington** See page 79.

**William Weatherford (Chief Red Eagle) (1780–1825)** led the Red Stick Creek Indians against the U.S. Army during the Creek War.

Hiram "Hank" Williams

Heather Whitestone

**Heather Whitestone (1973–)** was the first disabled woman chosen as Miss America. She was born in Dothan.

**Hiram "Hank" Williams (1923–1953)**, born in Mount Olive, began playing, singing, and writing his own songs in his early teens. When not in school, he played his Silvertone guitar on the sidewalk in front of Montgomery's WSFA radio station. Williams started a band, the Drifting Cowboys, that traveled from one small southern town to the next, playing at clubs and private parties. His songs include "I'm So Lonesome I Could Cry," "Your Cheatin' Heart," and "Take These Chains from My Heart."

**Edward O. Wilson (1929–)**, a two-time Pulitzer Prize winner, is a naturalist and entomologist on the faculty of Harvard University. He was born in Birmingham.

**Tammy Wynette (1942–1998)**, known as the First Lady of Country Music, sang such songs as "Stand By Your Man." She grew up on the Mississippi-Alabama border and lived for a time in Birmingham.

# RESOURCES

## BOOKS

### Nonfiction

Axelrod-Contrada, Joan. *Mia Hamm: Soccer Player*. New York: Ferguson Publishing Company, 2005.

Barrett, Tracy. *Trail of Tears: An American Tragedy*. Logan, Iowa: Perfection Learning, 2000.

Caravantes, Peggy. *Petticoat Spies: Six Women Spies of the Civil War*. Greensboro, N.C.: Morgan Reynolds, 2002.

DeCapua, Sarah. *The Tuskegee Airmen*. Chanhassen, Minn.: The Child's World, 2003.

Feeney, Kathy. *Alabama*. Danbury, Conn.: Children's Press, 2002.

Gibson, Karen Bush. *The Chickasaw Nation*. Mankato, Minn.: Bridgestone Books, 2002.

Martin, Michael A. *Alabama: The Heart of Dixie*. Milwaukee, Wisc.: Gareth Stevens Publishing, 2002.

Parks, Rosa, and Jim Haskins. *Rosa Parks: My Story*. New York: Puffin Books, 1999.

Pierce, Alan. *The Montgomery Bus Boycott*. Edina, Minn.: ABDO & Daughters, 2005.

Sorensen, Lita. *The Scottsboro Boys Trial: A Primary Source Account*. New York: Rosen Publishing, 2003.

Walker, Sally. *Secrets of a Civil War Submarine: Solving the Mysteries of the H. L. Hunley*. Minneapolis: Carolrhoda Books, 2005.

Wheeler, Jill C. *George Washington Carver*. Edina, Minn.: ABDO & Daughters, 2003.

### Fiction

Curtis, Christopher Paul. *The Watsons Go to Birmingham*. New York: Laurel Leaf, 2000.

Key, Watt. *Alabama Moon*. New York: Farrar, Straus, and Giroux, 2006.

McKissack, Patricia C. *Run Away Home*. New York: Scholastic, 2001.

Myers, Walter Dean. *The Journal of Biddy Owens: The Negro Leagues, Birmingham, Alabama, 1948*. New York: Scholastic, 2001.

# DVDs

*Crossing the Bridge.* A&E Home Video, 2006.
*Discoveries ... America: Alabama.* Bennett-Watt Entertainment, 2004.
*In Remembrance of Martin.* PBS Paramount, 2005.
*Scottsboro: Foul Play in the Bible Belt (City Confidential).* A&E Home Video, 2000.
*The Quiltmakers of Gee's Bend.* Alabama Public Television, 2005.
*The Tuskegee Airmen: They Fought Two Wars.* PBS Home Video, 2003.

# WEB SITES AND ORGANIZATIONS

**Alabama Bureau of Tourism & Travel**
*www.touralabama.org/*
Find information about tourist sites and cities.

**Alabama Department of Archives & History**
*www.archives.state.al.us*
An ideal site for finding primary source material about Alabama.

**Alabama State Department of Education**
*www.alsde.edu/*
Schools, curricula, statistics, and more about Alabama education.

**The Official Web Site of the State of Alabama**
*www.alabama.gov/*
To learn more information about the state government and online services.

# INDEX

★　★　★